ABOUT THE AUTHOR

Di Weiss's career has ranged from being a Special Needs Teacher to running her own company selling school software, but throughout she has been a passionate cook whose food delights family and friends.

Di is married to Oliver and the family spent some years living and working in Greece. They now live in London with Doug and Norman, the Labradors. Her three grown-up children are regular visitors, probably on account of the food.

DEDICATION

This is dedicated to the people I love most in the world: my husband, Oliver, my children, Tom, Patch and Jess, my daughters in law, Nikita and Sarah and my sisters, Jennifer and Elizabeth and my granddaughter, Daphne. Not forgetting the memory of my mother. She was a great cook and taught us to love cooking. My children, in turn, are fabulous, creative and enthusiastic cooks.

Finally, in memory of my dearest friends, Jillie, Diane and Christine – all amazing cooks and entertainers. And Charlie and Dennis, great entertainers – but not great cooks.

Di Weiss

SIMPLY NO WEIGH

AUSTIN MACAULEY PUBLISHERS™
LONDON • CAMBRIDGE • NEW YORK • SHARJAH

Copyright © Di Weiss (2018)

The right of Di Weiss to be identified as author of this work has been asserted by her in accordance with section 77 and 78 of the Copyright, Designs and Patents Act 1988.

All rights reserved. No part of this publication may be reproduced, stored in a retrieval system, or transmitted in any form or by any means, electronic, mechanical, photocopying, recording, or otherwise, without the prior permission of the publishers.

Any person who commits any unauthorised act in relation to this publication may be liable to criminal prosecution and civil claims for damages.

A CIP catalogue record for this title is available from the British Library.

ISBN 978-1-78823-672-0 (Paperback)
ISBN 978-1-78823-673-7 (Hardback)
ISBN 978-1-78823-674-3 (E-Book)
www.austinmacauley.com

First Published (2018)
Austin Macauley Publishers Ltd™
25 Canada Square
Canary Wharf
London
E14 5LQ

CREDITS

Photography: Yasmin Afshar
Styling: Miranda Stevenson
Illustrations: Daryl Stevenson

ACKNOWLEDGEMENTS

Where to start? To Miranda Stevenson for her incredible inspiration in styling the food for the photographic sessions, to Yasmin Afshar for her brilliant and creative photography and to Daryl Stevenson, a hugely talented artist. Their enthusiasm helped me to get this idea off the ground just when I thought I had hit a wall.

To Jane Kingsmill for her help with the written word.

And to friendship. To my many great friends too numerous to mention but for starters, the girls: Jen, Liz, Jess, Anna, Sarah, Jane, Jo, Louise, Margaret, Karen, Dee, Alison, Jan, Bev, Susan, Pauline, Angie, Alice, Sian, Robyn, Lou, Helen, Anne, Daryl, Michelle, Idina, Hils, Di, Christabel, Judy, Rosy, Menna, Amanda, Sue, Clare, Catriona, Ida, Diana, Debbie, Shirley, Trisha, Nikita, Sarah and Daphne.

To my children, Tom, Patch and Jess, for their support and patience in listening endlessly from the embryo of this idea to the completion. And, finally, to Oliver for tidying the kitchen after our photographic sessions. You are my backbone.

CONTENTS

BEGINNING 14
  Soups, Starters and Light Meals 14
    Bacon Quiche 16
    Goat's Cheese Tortilla 18
    Honey and Mustard Cocktail Sausages 20
    Onion Croustades 22
    Pea Bruschetta 24
    Smoked Salmon Blinis 26
    Spiced Pumpkin Soup 28
    Spinach Soup 30
    Tomato Bruschetta 32

MIDDLE 34
  Chicken 34
    Chicken with Cashew Nuts 36
    Chicken Pie 38
    Coq au Vin 40
    Chinese Chicken Stir Fry 42
    Jess's Thai 44
    Mild Chicken and Coriander Curry 46
    Moroccan Spiced Kebabs 48
    Roast Chicken 50
    Spicy Chicken with Lentils 52
    Tarragon Chicken 54
    Warm Chicken Salad 56
  Fish 58
    Asian Tuna 60
    Chilli Prawns 62
    Chilli Salmon Fishcakes 64
    Monkfish with Lentils 66

Prawn Stir Fry 68
Salmon Pesto 70
Salade Niçoise 72
Salmon and Black Bean Sauce 74
Spiced Cod 76

Pork and Ham 78
Barbequed Pork Kebabs 80
Gammon and Parsley Sauce 82
Paprika Pork 84
Patch's Pork 86
Pork Steaks with Caramelised Onions 90
Pork with Mushrooms, Onions and Garlic 92
Pork Steaks with Pak Choi 94
Toad in the Hole 96

Lamb 98
Brochettes of Lamb with Pesto 100
Butterflied Lamb 102
Greek Lamb Skewers 104
Harissa Lamb 106
Jen's Roast Lamb 108
Lamb Korma 110
Lamb Mince 112
Moussaka 114

Beef 116
Beef Goulash 118
Beef Stroganoff 120
Boeuf Bourguignon 122
Cottage Pie 126
Chilli Beef 128
Chilli Con Carne 130
Dee's Cumberland Pie 132
Lasagne 134
Meatballs 136
Mince 138
Tom's Chilli Burgers 140

END 142

Puddings and Desserts 142

- Apple Crumble 144
- Baked Alaska 146
- Baked Custard 148
- Cheese Cake 150
- Chocolate Biscuit Cake 152
- Chocolate Mousse 154
- Fruit Strudel 156
- Lemon Mousse 158
- Speedy Lemon Flan 160
- Summer Pudding 162
- Raspberry Ice Cream 164
- Raspberry Coulis 166
- Warm Fruit Salad 168
- White Chocolate and Raspberry Tart 170

IN-BETWEEN 172

Salads and Veg 172

- Bacon and Tomato Salad 174
- Coleslaw 176
- Honey and Lemon Couscous 177
- Leek Gratin 178
- Lots of Beans Salad 180
- Mushy Peas 182
- Potato and Celeriac Mash 183
- Pumpkin with Lime and Yoghurt 184
- Red Cabbage 186
- Roasted Med Veg 188
- Roasted Tomato and Mozzarella Salad 190
- Rosemary and Garlic Roasted Potatoes 192
- Sesame Seed Salad 194
- Tarragon Carrots 196
- Tasty Rice 198

Sauces 200
    Apple and Mustard Sauce 202
    Béarnaise Sauce with Tarragon.. 204
    Cheese Sauce 206
    Exceedingly Easy Parsley Sauce.. 207
    Guacamole... 208
    Hollandaise Sauce.. 210
    Liz's Mango Salsa... 212
    Mushroom Sauce 214
    Onion Gravy.. 216
    Port and Cranberry Sauce 217
    Tomato and Onion Relish 218
    Red Pepper Sauce 219
    Satay Sauce... 220
    Tartare Sauce 222
    Tomato Sauce 223
    Tzatziki 224

*Every story has a beginning,
a middle and an end...*

...and an in-between.

BEGINNING

SOUPS, STARTERS AND LIGHT MEALS

Bacon Quiche

Goat's Cheese Tortilla

Honey and Mustard Cocktail Sausages

Onion Croustades

Pea Bruschetta

Smoked Salmon Blinis

Spiced Pumpkin Soup

Spinach Soup

Tomato Bruschetta

BACON QUICHE

Ingredients

1 pack frozen shortcrust pastry (defrosted)
2 tablespoons of olive oil
Scoop of butter
4 eggs
8 rashers of streaky bacon – cut into strips
1 large onion, peeled and diced
4 heaped tablespoons of crème fraîche (approx. 400 ml)
3 heaped tablespoons of Gruyère cheese
10 baby tomatoes, halved

Equipment

Loose-bottomed tin (approx. 24 cm)
Oven: 200°C, 180°C fan, Gas Mark 6
Baking beans
Greaseproof paper

▎*Tips and Tricks*

Baking beans are worth the investment, but if you don't have any, you can sprinkle a good couple of handfuls of uncooked rice instead onto the greaseproof paper.

What to Do

1. Roll out the pastry on a clean, floured work surface, line the tin, trim the edges and prick the base about 6 times with a fork.
2. Cover the pastry with greaseproof paper and weigh down with baking beans or uncooked rice if you don't have baking beans, and bake in the preheated oven for 10 minutes.
3. In the meantime, put the olive oil and butter in the frying pan, and when it's sizzling, chuck in the diced bacon and onions.
4. Gently fry for about 5 minutes until it's just beginning to brown and stir frequently to prevent it from sticking.
5. Take the tin out of the oven and remove the paper and the beans, and bake for a further 15 minutes until just golden and set aside.
6. Beat the eggs with the crème fraîche, add the grated cheese, bacon and onion mixture, top with halves of the baby tomatoes, sliced side up and pour into the pastry case.
7. Bake for 30 minutes until the mixture has risen but still a bit 'wobbly'.
8. Allow the quiche to cool and slightly set before serving.
9. Baking the base crisps it up – once the egg mixture is added, the pastry base stops cooking – so make sure it looks almost done before adding the egg mixture.

Serves 4

GOAT'S CHEESE TORTILLA

Ingredients

1 large sweet potato – peeled and sliced
1 large onion – peeled and sliced
1 fennel bulb – sliced
1 red pepper – cored and sliced
1 yellow pepper – cored and sliced
2 tablespoons of olive oil
3 eggs
Small carton of single cream
Splash of milk
1 pack of crumbly goat's cheese
½ a pack of Taleggio cheese (about 125g)
1 tablespoon of Gruyère
2 good handfuls of spinach leaves

Equipment

Oven: 220°C, 200°C fan, Gas Mark 7
Hob
20 cm cake tin with removable bottom
Electric whisk

■ *Tips and Tricks*

If you can't find Taleggio cheese – add an extra tablespoon of Gruyère.

What to Do

1. Drizzle the oil over the sweet potatoes, peppers, onions and fennel and roast for 30 minutes in the preheated oven on the high heat until they are tender and just beginning to turn golden brown.
2. Remove from the oven and set aside.
3. Reduce the oven to 170°C, 150°C fan and Gas Mark 3.
4. Meanwhile, whisk together the eggs, cream and a splash of milk and throw in the grated Gruyère, goat's cheese and Taleggio, roughly chopped.
5. Put the roasted vegetables and uncooked spinach in a 20 cm cake tin with a removable bottom and pour over the egg and cheese mixture.
6. Cook in the oven for an hour or until golden brown and set.
7. Serve hot – or at room temperature.

This is great for vegetarians – or as a light lunch with a green salad.

It looks like a lot of ingredients, but the end result is worth it.

Serves 4

HONEY AND MUSTARD COCKTAIL SAUSAGES

Ingredients

24 cocktail sausages (allow at least 4 per person)
1 tablespoon of runny honey
1 dessertspoon of grainy mustard
Small wooden cocktail sticks

Equipment

Medium hot grill – preheated

▋*Tips and Tricks*

To prepare ahead – slightly reduce the cooking time of the sausages and just before serving put them back into a preheated medium oven for about 5 minutes – before putting in the cocktail sticks.

What to Do

1. Mix together the honey and mustard in a bowl and then coat the sausages with the mixture.
2. Grill the sausages – turning at least once – for about 10 minutes until golden brown and cooked evenly – but keep your eye on them as the honey can make them scorch.
3. Spike each sausage with a cocktail stick – and serve with mustard and tomato ketchup.
4. Allow at least 4 sausages per head.

ONION CROUSTADES

Ingredients

- 1 pack of 24 Croustades
- 1 tablespoon of olive oil
- 1 large onion – finely chopped
- 1 dessertspoon of soft brown sugar
- 1 tablespoon of Balsamic vinegar
- 1 pack of crumbly goat's cheese
- 8 cherry tomatoes

▍*Tips and Tricks*

If you can't find ready-made Croustades – thinly slice a French loaf, and put the slices into a preheated oven (200°C, 180°C fan, Gas Mark 5) for about 5 or 6 minutes until they are crispy. Make a base of the goat's cheese, onions on top and then the tomatoes. It's better this way – or the onions will topple off.

Equipment

Hob
Baking tray
Oven: 200°C, 180°C fan, Gas Mark 6

What to Do

1. Heat the oil in a pan and add the finely chopped onions and cook for about 5 minutes.
2. Add the Balsamic vinegar and brown sugar and cook for another 5 minutes until the onions are softening and the mixture is slightly sticky.
3. Put a little of the onion mixture into each Croustade with a tiny layer of goat's cheese and top with a quarter of cherry tomato.
4. Put them onto a baking tray and heat for about 5 minutes and serve straight away.
5. You can't fill the Croustades more than 10 or 15 minutes in advance as they will go soggy – but they go down a storm.

Serves 6

PEA BRUSCHETTA

Ingredients

1 medium French loaf
Scoop of butter
½ small pack of frozen peas (about 250 g)
6/8 spring onions – chopped
1 heaped tablespoon of cream cheese
1 tablespoon of shaved Parmesan cheese
A few sprigs of mint

Equipment

Hob
Grill
Blender

■ Tips and Tricks

You can prepare the toast ahead – but put the mixture on not more than 20 minutes before – or like the tomato version on page 32 it will go soggy.

What to Do

1 Thinly slice the French loaf – allowing at least 4 slices per person – lightly toast each side and set aside.
2 Heat up the butter in a saucepan, add the chopped spring onions when it's just sizzling, and fry for about 5 minutes until they are just beginning to soften.
3 Add the frozen peas to the pan with 2/3 tablespoons of water. Season and continue cooking for a few minutes, until the mixture is just simmering.
4 Take the pan off the heat, add the cream cheese and put the mixture into the blender.
5 Spread it on the toast just before serving, grate the Parmesan on top and garnish with a few sprigs of mint.
6 This is a variation of my favourite, Tomato Bruschetta – and looks effective if you serve the 2 together.

Allow about 4 slices per person

SMOKED SALMON BLINIS

Ingredients

16 blinis
1 pack of smoked salmon (about 200 g) – preferably wild or organic
1 small tub of crème fraîche or natural yoghurt
Small jar of lumpfish caviar
1 lemon
Grated pepper

Equipment

Medium grill

▌ *Tips and Tricks*

The better the salmon – the better this is. Avoid the over-coloured cheap salmon that looks artificial and tastes like engine oil.

What to Do

1. Grill the blinis under a preheated grill for about a minute each side until slightly 'toasted'.
2. Allow them to cool.
3. Just before serving, put a teaspoon of crème fraîche on the blinis, a curl of smoked salmon and top with the lumpfish caviar.
4. Add a squeeze of lemon and freshly ground black pepper.
5. These look great, taste fantastic and always impress the guests.

Allow about 4 per person

SPICED PUMPKIN SOUP

Ingredients

1 small pumpkin
3 tablespoons of olive oil
Scoop of butter
2 sticks of celery – chopped
2 large onions – peeled and chopped
2 teaspoons of ground cumin
2 teaspoons of ground coriander
3 tablespoons of coconut milk or natural yoghurt
2-3 mugs of vegetable stock
Water

Tips and Tricks

If you want a more powerful brew – go for it and chuck in more cumin and coriander –tasting as you go. If it looks a bit too thick – put in a splash of water or a bit more stock.

Equipment

Hob
Oven: 200°C, 180°C fan or Gas Mark 6

What to Do

1. Take the head and tail off the pumpkin, leave on the skin, cut into quarters and scoop out the seeds.
2. Put the pumpkin into a baking tray and sprinkle with half of the olive oil, salt and pepper and roast for 30-40 minutes.
3. When it is soft, scoop out the flesh and discard the skin.
4. While the pumpkin is in the oven, heat the remaining olive oil and a scoop of butter in a pan and add the chopped onion and celery, and fry for about 5 or 6 minutes until just beginning to soften.
5. When the pumpkin is ready, add it to the pan with the onions and celery and add the stock, cumin, coriander and coconut milk (or yoghurt).
6. Bring gently to simmering point.
7. Put the mixture into a food processor and blend until smooth.
8. Return to the pan and heat.
9. Check the seasoning and serve with crusty bread.

This mildly spicy soup can also be made with butternut squash (a small one), 5/6 large parsnips or 7/8 large carrots. The spices add fragrance – not heat.

Serves 4-6

SPINACH SOUP

Ingredients

Generous scoop of butter
1 large onion – chopped
2 sticks of celery – chopped
2 medium potatoes – peeled and roughly   chopped
1 litre vegetable stock
1 medium bag of baby leaf spinach
2 tablespoons of Crème fraîche
Snipped chives

Equipment

Hob
Blender

■ Tips and Tricks

Ring the changes and swap the spinach with 2 large, washed and roughly chopped leeks or courgettes, but add them to the pan with the potatoes.

What to Do

1. Melt the butter in a large saucepan, and add the peeled, chopped potatoes, sliced celery and chopped onions and fry very gently for about 10-15 minutes until just turning golden.
2. Pour in half the stock and simmer for 15 minutes, until the potatoes are very soft.
3. Add the spinach and cook for a further 2 minutes until wilted.
4. Put into a blender and whizz up until smooth.
5. Return the soup to the pan, and add the remaining stock until it's a consistency you like.
6. Swirl in the crème fraîche and snipped chives just before serving.

Serves 4

TOMATO BRUSCHETTA

Ingredients

1 medium French loaf
6 medium ripe tomatoes
3 tablespoons of olive oil
¼ teaspoon of sugar
2 cloves of garlic – crushed
Salt and pepper
Fresh basil leaves

▎*Tips and Tricks*

If you're short of time – don't skin the tomatoes – just chop them up with their skins on.

Equipment

Grill/Toaster

What to do

1. Put the tomatoes in a bowl and cover with boiling water, slash with a knife and leave for a minute or two until the skin peels off with your thumb. Don't leave them in the water too long – or they 'cook'.
2. Chop the tomatoes roughly, removing the core, drain off the excess liquid and add 2 tablespoons of the olive oil, sugar, salt, pepper and crushed garlic.
3. Meanwhile, cut the French loaf into thin slices – allowing at least four slices per person – and lightly toast both sides.
4. Just before serving, put a generous spoonful of the tomato mixture on each slice of toast, drizzle with the remaining oil and tear up the basil leaves to scatter on top.

Allow at least one tomato per person. The tomato mixture can be made in advance and refrigerated – but don't put it on the toast too early – or it will go soggy.

This is so simple – and absolutely delicious. I serve it with drinks before dinner – or double up the quantities and serve as a light lunch with cheese.

Allow 3-4 slices each

BEGINNING: SOUPS, STARTERS AND LIGHT MEALS

MIDDLE

CHICKEN

Chicken with Cashew Nuts
Chicken Pie
Coq au Vin
Chinese Chicken Stir Fry
Jess's Thai Green
Mild Curry and Coriander
Moroccan Spiced Kebabs
Roast Chicken
Spicy Chicken with Lentils
Tarragon Chicken
Warm Chicken Salad

CHICKEN WITH CASHEW NUTS

Ingredients

4 medium chicken breasts – cut into 4 slices
1 large onion – chopped
1 dessertspoon of fresh ginger – peeled and grated
2 level teaspoons of ground turmeric
2 cloves of garlic – crushed
2 heaped tablespoons of cashew nuts
1 level tablespoon of curry paste
½ large tub of natural yoghurt – reserving 1 tablespoon for garnish
2 lemons – juice and zest of 1 – and the other for garnish
Handful of chopped parsley – optional

■ *Tips and Tricks*

Curry paste comes in various strengths – so, go for mild if you don't like it too hot. You can marinade this the day before and keep refrigerated until you're ready to start cooking.

Equipment

    Hob
    Large oven-proof pan
    Blender

What to Do

1 Chop the onion, peel and grate the ginger and put them into the blender with the turmeric, curry paste, garlic, yoghurt (leaving a tablespoon or 2 for garnish), zest and juice of 1 lemon, and blend to a smooth paste.
2 Coat the chicken with the paste and put in a non-metallic dish, cover and marinade for 3 hours, or preferably overnight – in the fridge.
3 Take the chicken and marinade out of the dish and transfer to a pan, add a wineglass of water and the cashew nuts, and bring very gently to simmering point. Add another splash of water if it looks too dry.
4 Continue to simmer on a very low heat for about 20 minutes until the chicken is cooked through and tender.
5 When you're ready to serve, spoon a little of the reserved yoghurt on top of the chicken and garnish with some chopped parsley and a slice of lemon.
6 Serve with plain rice or naan bread, mango chutney and a salad.

Serves 4

CHICKEN PIE

Ingredients

12 boneless chicken thighs
2 scoops of butter
2 medium carrots – peeled and sliced
2 medium sticks of celery – washed and sliced
2 medium leeks – washed and sliced
1 tablespoon of olive oil
8 medium-sized button mushrooms
2 tablespoons of flour
2 teaspoons of grainy mustard
2 mugs of milk
1 mug of chicken or vegetable stock
1 glass of white wine
1 tablespoon of tarragon or thyme – chopped
1 egg for glazing
1 pack of frozen puff pastry – defrosted

Equipment

Hob
Oven: 200°C, 180°C fan, Gas Mark 6
Large saucepan
Deep oven-proof dish

Tips and Tricks

You can make the chicken the day before, keep it in the fridge and top with the pastry just before you put it in the oven.

What to Do

1. Cut up the chicken thighs into 'bite-sized' pieces.
2. Heat the olive oil and the butter in the pan and when just sizzling, add the chicken, carrots, leeks and celery and cook for about 10 minutes, stirring continuously until just turning golden brown.
3. Take the pan off the hob, and stir in the flour.
4. Add the mustard, wine and milk, return to the heat and bring the mixture very slowly to simmering point, and keep stirring until it thickens. If it looks too thick – add another splash of milk.
5. Add the chopped tarragon and season to taste.
6. Put the chicken into an oven-proof dish, and set aside to cool.
7. Dust a clean work surface with flour and roll out the puff pastry to fit the oven-proof dish. Gently lay the pastry on the chicken mixture, pressing the pastry to the side of the dish with the tip of a knife to seal it. Brush with beaten egg and prick with a fork to allow the steam to escape.
8. Cook in the preheated oven for 30-40 minutes until the pastry is well-risen and golden.

I always use chicken thighs, not breasts, for this recipe. They don't look quite as pretty but are always tender and much cheaper. All this needs is frozen peas.

Serves 4-6

COQ AU VIN

Ingredients

8 chicken joints – a selection of breasts, thighs and legs – on the bone
2 tablespoons of olive oil
2 tablespoons of flour
Generous scoop of butter
10 slices of streaky bacon
2 glasses of red wine
2 large onions
10-12 button mushrooms
2 carrots (sliced)
3 cloves of garlic (crushed)
2 bouquet garni
10 baby onions – peeled
Pinch of sugar
Handful of fresh herbs – thyme, tarragon or rosemary
1 dessertspoon of redcurrant jelly
2 or 3 mugs of hot stock (chicken or vegetable)

Equipment

Large flameproof casserole dish
Hob
Oven: 160°C, 140°C fan, Gas Mark 3

■ *Tips and Tricks*

If you like to cook ahead, this dish is perfect. In fact, it actually improves if you make it the day before. Cool and refrigerate overnight and then re-heat in a medium oven for about 45 minutes until it's piping hot. Add the mushrooms and shallots too at this stage.

A good trick to prevent weepy eyes when peeling the baby onions is to put them in a heatproof basin, pour over a kettle of boiling water and leave for 2 or 3 minutes. They are then much easier to peel.

What to Do

1. Coat the chicken with the flour.
2. Heat the olive oil and butter in a large flameproof casserole dish on the hob. When the oil is sizzling add the joints – half at a time to allow the joints to brown and not steam – and cook until just golden for approximately 5 minutes each side. Remove the first batch of chicken and repeat with the remaining joints. Set them aside.
3. Add an extra glug of olive oil to the pan and fry the chopped onion, diced bacon and sliced carrot, and cook on a medium heat until just soft and then stir in the crushed garlic.
4. Put the chicken back into the casserole dish with the vegetables and add the red wine and stock, bouquet garni and a pinch of sugar, along with the redcurrant jelly.
5. Put the casserole dish into the preheated oven with the lid on, and cook slowly for 2½-3 hours until the chicken is falling off the bone.
6. In the meantime, peel the baby onions and sauté them in a frying pan with a splash of olive oil for about 10 minutes, shaking the pan continuously so they don't scorch – and set aside.
7. Fry the mushrooms in the same pan for a few minutes – and set aside with the baby onions. Allow to cool.
8. Keep checking the oven and make sure the chicken is well covered with the stock, wine and vegetables.
9. Add the mushrooms and shallots 45 minutes before the end of the cooking time, and return to the oven.

Don't be put off by the long list of ingredients – once it's cooked it looks after itself – and it's brilliant for entertaining. Mashed spud is best with this to soak up the juices.

I think most recipes underestimate the time for cooking coq au vin. So long as the lid is on the pan in the oven at a gentle heat, and there's plenty of liquid, I say the longer, the better – but check every so often – and add a bit more stock or wine if it looks as if it's drying out.

Serves 4-6

CHINESE CHICKEN STIR FRY

Ingredients

4 chicken breasts – sliced
1 tablespoon of flour
1 dessertspoon of Chinese Five Spice
2 tablespoons of olive oil
½ teaspoon of mild chilli powder
1 lemon – juice and zest
1 piece Chinese Stem Ginger – in a jar
1 tablespoon of Stem Ginger Syrup
Selection of stir fry vegetables: broccoli, mange touts, spring onions, baby corn, and red peppers.

Equipment

Wok
Hob

■ *Tips and Tricks*

If you're using dried noodles – begin cooking them when you start cooking the chicken.

What to Do

1. Mix together the flour, chilli powder and Chinese Five Spice powder in a plastic bag, add the chicken and toss to coat evenly.
2. Heat half the oil in a wok until sizzling and then add the chicken, and fry for about 6 or 7 minutes until it's golden brown and cooked through – check it's not pink in the middle. Cover and keep warm in the oven.
3. Wipe the wok with kitchen paper, and add the remaining oil, heat until sizzling and then throw in the vegetables and cook for a further 2 minutes on high heat until they are hot but still crispy.
4. Return the chicken to the pan with the vegetables and add the lemon zest and juice, the chopped stem ginger and 2 tablespoons of stem ginger syrup.
5. Add a tablespoon of water if the mixture looks too thick.
6. Serve with noodles and a green salad.

Fresh noodles work best with this stir fry – as they only need minutes before serving.

Serves 4

JESS'S THAI

Ingredients

12 skinless boned chicken thighs – cubed
1 tablespoon of olive oil
Bunch of spring onions
2 cloves of garlic – crushed
2 lemongrass stalks – roughly chopped
1 dessertspoon of grated ginger
1 teaspoon of ground cumin
1 large green chilli – seeded
1 bunch of coriander
1 tablespoon of fish sauce
½ tin of coconut milk
1 chicken or vegetable stock cube
1 pack of green beans, topped and tailed

Equipment

Wok
Hob
Blender

■ *Tips and Tricks*

If it's too 'pokey' for your liking, add the remainder of the coconut milk a little at a time to tame it.

Chicken thighs work so well with this recipe. I often find chicken breasts end up tough if you cook them on too high heat. Thighs are much less temperamental.

What to Do

1. Make the curry paste by blitzing the garlic, lemongrass, ginger, cumin, deseeded green chilli, fish sauce and half of the bunch of fresh coriander in the blender.
2. Heat the oil in the wok, add the chopped spring onions and the chicken, and cook for 6 or 7 minutes until just turning golden.
3. Add the curry paste to the wok and cook for another 5 minutes.
4. Pour in the coconut milk and the crumbled stock cube into the wok and bring gently to simmering point, and continue to cook for another 15 minutes.
5. Add about a mug of water and the green beans and cook for another 5 minutes.
6. Make sure the chicken is cooked through and hot, and check the seasoning.

This is one of my daughter Jess's 'signature dishes'. She's experimented with various combinations of recipes and has perfected this.

All this needs is rice.

Serves 4

MILD CHICKEN AND CORIANDER CURRY

Ingredients

4 boneless chicken breasts – sliced
2 tablespoons of olive oil
2 level tablespoons of mild curry paste
1 large onion – chopped
1 sweet potato – peeled and roughly chopped
½ can of coconut milk
1 can of chopped tomatoes
Large handful of chopped, fresh coriander

Equipment

Hob
Wok

■ Tips and Tricks

If this is too mild – put in another tablespoon of curry paste – or use medium instead of mild curry paste.

What to Do

1. Heat the olive oil in the wok, add the chopped onions and sweet potato and fry gently for about 10 minutes before chucking in the sliced chicken breasts.
2. Continue cooking slowly for a few more minutes and then add the curry paste.
3. Stir in the coconut milk and tinned tomatoes and simmer very gently for 20 minutes.
4. Just before serving, add the chopped coriander and stir in so it's just beginning to wilt.

This one-pan dish is speedy and much nicer than most ready-made supermarket versions. For added virtue – use half-fat coconut milk.

Serve with rice or naan bread and mango chutney.

Serves 4

MOROCCAN SPICED KEBABS

Ingredients

4 skinless chicken breasts – cut into chunks
2 onions – peeled and quartered
1 red pepper – roughly cubed and de-seeded
1 yellow pepper – roughly cubed and de-seeded
2 garlic cloves
1 teaspoon of paprika
1 teaspoon of cumin
2 tablespoons of chopped parsley
1 teaspoon of ground coriander
Zest and juice of 1 lemon
Squidge of honey
2 small tubs of natural yoghurt
Small bunch of mint – chopped
2 tablespoons of olive oil

Equipment

Blender
Grill – medium heat or barbeque
Kebab sticks

■ Tips and Tricks

If you're using wooden kebab sticks, soak them in water for a good few hours so they don't burn – but I think the metal ones are way better.

Leaving the chicken to marinate really helps it soak up the flavours and the yoghurt makes it extra tender.

What to Do

1. Put the paprika, cumin, parsley, coriander, zest and juice of the lemon, honey and 1 tub of yoghurt (reserving the other for garnish) into a blender and whiz to make a paste.
2. Cut the chicken into cubes and rub the paste over the chicken and leave to marinate. Cover and chill for a few hours or, preferably, overnight in the fridge.
3. Just before cooking, thread the chicken, onions and peppers onto the kebab sticks.
4. Preheat the grill to medium, and grill for about 8 minutes each side but check it's cooked right through and not pink inside. If you're barbequing – make sure you light it in good time.

This is a great dish for the barbeque. Chicken off the bone is much better than joints that tend to be 'carbonara' on the outside and pink inside.

Serve this with tzatziki (page 224), mango chutney and sprinkle with the chopped mint. If you have time, you can make Liz's Mango Salsa instead on page 212 and Satay Sauce on page 220. This combination is a fabulous mix of flavours.

I love these kebabs with pita bread. Take the chicken off the kebab sticks and pile it into a warmed pita, a dollop of natural yoghurt and sprinkle with the chopped mint.

Serves 4

ROAST CHICKEN

Ingredients

1 medium whole chicken – preferably free range
1 tablespoon of runny honey
2 teaspoons of grainy mustard
1 tablespoon of olive oil
1 lemon – zest and juice
8 rashers of streaky bacon
1 onion
Handful of herbs – thyme or tarragon

For the gravy

1 tablespoon of flour
1 glass of red wine
2/3 mugs of stock
1 dessertspoon of redcurrant jelly
Splash of soy sauce
1 tablespoon of tomato puree

Equipment

Oven: 200°C, 180°C fan, Gas Mark 6
Roasting tin

▌*Tips and Tricks*

For roast chicken – get the very best you can afford – it makes all the difference.

If your gravy is lumpy – don't panic – just put it through a sieve and pour it into a warmed jug.

What to Do

1. Preheat the oven.
2. Mix together the olive oil, the juice and zest of the lemon, (reserving the skins), the grainy mustard and the honey.
3. Spread the mixture over the chicken.
4. Put the tarragon or thyme, onion and the squeezed lemons into the cavity of the chicken.
5. Put into the hot oven and cook for 15 minutes on high heat and then turn the heat down to 180°C, 160°C fan, Gas Mark 4 and roast for at least another 1¼ hours.
6. If you're using bacon, lay the rashers on top of the chicken 20 minutes before you take it out of the oven – so it's crispy but not scorched to a cinder.
7. Put a sharp knife into the leg of the chicken and if the juices run clear – it's cooked. If not – put it back for another 15 minutes and check again.
8. Dish onto a serving plate to rest, cover and keep warm while you make the gravy.
9. Drain off the fat from the roasting tin – leaving about a tablespoon in the bottom. Put the flour into the roasting tin with the cooking juices and stir in to combine.
10. When there are no lumps, pour in the wine, the soy sauce and the stock and cook for a few minutes on the hob until it's thickened, and then add a spoonful of redcurrant jelly and the tomato puree.
11. Check for seasoning – if it needs more oomph – add a bit more soy sauce, another splash of wine and a sprinkling of stock powder.

All this needs is garlic and rosemary roast potatoes (page 192), a green veg and if you're feeling energetic, tarragon carrots on page 196.

This is classic roast chicken with a twist. The lemons, herbs, honey and mustard give this recipe some extra zip.

Serves 4-6

SPICY CHICKEN WITH LENTILS

Ingredients

4 chicken breasts
2 teaspoons of ground cumin
2 teaspoons of ground coriander
2 lemons – zest and juice
2 tablespoons of olive oil
2 onions – peeled and chopped
4 or 5 medium carrots – peeled and sliced
1 tablespoon of tomato purée
2 mugs of hot chicken stock
1 tin of lentils
1-2 teaspoons of harissa paste
2 tablespoons of hummus for serving
1 teaspoon of paprika
Handful of chopped parsley

Equipment

Grill – medium heat
Wok or frying pan
Hob

▌ *Tips and Tricks*

This is as delicious with green salad, warmed pita bread and a glass of white wine on a hot day as it is in the winter with a glass of Merlot. If you don't feel like spicy – leave out the harissa paste.

What to Do

1. Mix the cumin and coriander with the zest and juice from 1 lemon, and 1 tablespoon of oil to make a paste to coat the chicken.
2. Leave it to marinate in the fridge for an hour or 2, or if you have time – preferably overnight.
3. Rinse and drain the lentils, heat up the remaining tablespoons of olive oil in the wok and add the onions and carrots, and sauté gently for 6-7 minutes before adding the stock, lentils, tomato purée and harissa paste.
4. Simmer for 3 or 4 minutes until the stock is slightly absorbed.
5. Remove the wok from the heat, and cover the pan to keep it warm.
6. Grill the chicken under a medium grill for about 6 minutes each side. Pierce with a knife and if the juices are still pink, return to the grill for another minute or 2.
7. Make sure the lentil mixture is still hot and, if not, give it a gentle heat up.
8. Add the lentils to a warmed serving dish, put the chicken on top with a generous dollop of hummus on each bit, and sprinkle with the paprika and grated lemon zest.

Serves 4

TARRAGON CHICKEN

Ingredients

4 chicken breasts – skinned and sliced
1 dessertspoon of plain flour
1 tablespoon of olive oil
Scoop of butter
1 glass of white wine or chicken stock
1 tablespoon of single cream or natural yoghurt
2 teaspoons of grainy mustard
Large handful of fresh tarragon
1 large onion – peeled and sliced
6-8 medium mushrooms – sliced

Equipment

Hob
Wok or large saucepan

Tips and Tricks

Rice or noodles are perfect with this and a green salad – nothing more.

What to Do

1. Heat the oil in a wok or frying pan, add the onions when it's sizzling and cook for 3-4 minutes to soften.
2. Add the butter to the pan and chuck in the chicken and cook through gently for 5 or 6 minutes.
3. Keep the heat low or the butter scalds and tastes bitter.
4. Take the pan off the heat, stir in the flour and then return to the heat for a minute, stirring continuously, before adding the mustard, the wine or stock and the sliced mushrooms.
5. Bubble very gently for 15-20 minutes until the chicken is cooked through, stir in the cream or yoghurt and tarragon and heat through for a minute or 2 before serving.

A classic French dish – fresh tarragon and cream complement the chicken. If you've looked at the other chicken recipes of mine, you will realise I love 'spicy' – but I adore the combination of chicken and tarragon. A marriage made in heaven.

Serves 4

WARM CHICKEN SALAD

Ingredients

2 tablespoons of olive oil
1 lemon (zest and juice)
4 chicken breasts (cut into strips)
1 bag of mixed salad
2 sticks of celery – finely sliced
½ cucumber – sliced
2 teaspoons of white wine vinegar
1 teaspoon of runny honey
1 dessertspoon of sesame seeds (optional)

Equipment

Frying pan or wok
Hob

■ Tips and Tricks

For a different twist, use the zest and juice of half an orange.

What to Do

1. Put the salad, cucumber and celery in a large salad bowl.
2. Grate and squeeze the lemon and sprinkle the zest over the sliced chicken – reserving the juice.
3. Heat 1 tablespoon of olive oil in a pan and add the chicken when sizzling. Cook the chicken, flipping it over until golden brown and cooked through. This should take about 6-8 minutes depending on the thickness of the strips.
4. Transfer the chicken to a serving dish, cover and keep it warm.
5. Keep the cooking juices in the pan, and add the lemon juice, vinegar, remaining tablespoon of olive oil and the honey and bring gently to the boil.
6. Put the cooked chicken on top of the salad, tip the warm dressing over the mixture and serve immediately.

Salads don't have to be cool, crisp and sidelined by the main course. This one takes centre stage.

Serves 4

Asian Tuna

Chilli Prawns

Chilli Salmon Fishcakes

Monkfish with Lentils

Prawn Stir Fry

Salmon Pesto

Salade Niçoise

Salmon and Black Bean Sauce

Spiced Cod

ASIAN TUNA

Ingredients

    4 fresh tuna steaks
    1 dessertspoon of ginger (peeled and grated)
    6 spring onions – sliced
    1 dessertspoon of fish sauce
    1 tablespoon of oyster sauce
    2 tablespoons of soy sauce
    Juice of 1 lemon
    2 heads of pak choi or broccoli
    1 small red chilli – deseeded and finely chopped (optional)

■ *Tips and Tricks*

If you can't find tuna – monkfish or halibut works just as well.

Equipment

Oven-proof dish
Oven: 190°C, 170°C fan, Gas Mark 5

What to Do

1 Combine the ginger, fish sauce, oyster sauce, soy sauce and lemon juice in a bowl and add the chopped spring onions and pak choi or cabbage and the chilli, if you're using it.
2 Put the fish in a large sheet of tin foil, pour over the mixture with 3-4 tablespoons of water, and seal up.
3 Put on a baking tray in a preheated oven and bake for 20 minutes until cooked through.

Serve this with rice or rice noodles and sesame seed salad on page 194.

Serves 4

CHILLI PRAWNS

Ingredients

1 kg raw peeled prawns
1 large onion, peeled and chopped
1 pack of mangetout or sugar snap peas
1 teaspoon ground turmeric
½ teaspoon of chilli powder
1 tablespoon of olive oil
2 cloves of crushed garlic
1 green or red chilli – if you want super-hot
Handful of chopped coriander
2 limes

Equipment

Hob
Wok

■ Tips and Tricks

Similar to Prawn Stir Fry on page 68 but this has more of a curry flavour.

What to Do

1. Put the prawns in a bowl and sprinkle them with the turmeric, chilli powder and zest and juice of 1 lime (keep the other one for garnish).
2. Heat the oil in a wok and when sizzling, add the chopped onion and cook for 5 minutes or until it's just softening and then add the crushed garlic and chilli, if you are using it.
3. Toss in the prawns and cook until they turn pink and are hot through (round about 5 minutes) – but it slightly depends on how crowded the wok is – and then add the mangetout or sugar snap peas and continue cooking for another 2 minutes.
4. Add the chopped coriander just before serving and garnish with the second lime.
5. Serve with rice and a spoonful of mango chutney.

Serves 4-6

CHILLI SALMON FISHCAKES

Ingredients

4 salmon steaks – skinned
4-5 tablespoons of olive oil
1 small red chilli – deseeded and chopped
1 teaspoon of chilli flakes (optional)
1 dessertspoon of peeled and grated ginger
1 heaped tablespoon of breadcrumbs
1 egg – beaten
6 spring onions – chopped
2 teaspoons of grainy mustard
1 tablespoon of flour – for coating
2 limes

Equipment

Hob
Frying pan
Blender

■ Tips and Tricks

Serve with tzatziki on page 224, sesame salad page 194 and ready-made sweet chilli dipping sauce.

What to Do

1. Blend the spring onions, mustard, chilli, ginger, beaten egg and breadcrumbs in a food processor for about 15 seconds – until the spring onions are finely chopped.
2. Then add the salmon and pulse it to form a 'chunky' mixture – don't purée it.
3. Divide the mixture evenly into 8, roll each one into a ball and then flatten them to make a hamburger shape.
4. Put the flour on a clean work surface and coat the fishcakes with it.
5. Heat a frying pan with a tablespoon of olive oil and sauté the fishcakes for at least 4 minutes each side – until golden brown and hot right through.

These are closer to Thai fishcakes than the British kind – mash free and very light.

Serves 4

MONKFISH WITH LENTILS

Ingredients

4 monkfish fillets
2 tablespoons of olive oil
2 sticks of celery
1 large onion – chopped
2 carrots – peeled and chopped
1 tin or carton of lentils – drained and rinsed
12 sun-dried tomatoes from a jar – chopped
1 mug of chicken stock
8 slices of Parma ham
2 lemons

Equipment

Oven: 200°C, 180°C fan and Gas Mark 6
Roasting tin
Frying pan or wok

■ *Tips and Tricks*

Monkfish has a firm texture that stands up well to roasting, but you could use cod loin or halibut instead.

What to Do

1 Put the roasting tin in the preheated oven with a glug of olive oil.
2 Sprinkle the monkfish fillets with the juice of 1 lemon and a splash of olive oil. Wrap 2 slices of Parma ham around each fillet and put them in the roasting tin and roast for about 15-20 minutes.
3 Meanwhile, heat the remaining olive oil in the frying pan and when it's sizzling, add the onion, celery and carrots. Continue cooking for about 5 minutes before adding the lentils, sun-dried tomatoes and stock. Bring to simmering point and cook gently while the fish is roasting.
4 Put the lentils into a warmed serving dish and top with the fish – and garnish with the remaining lemon.

The lentils are easy to throw together – and the sun-dried tomatoes add richness to the flavour. No need for rice or spuds – just serve with a green salad.

Serves 4

PRAWN STIR FRY

Ingredients

2 tablespoons of sesame oil or olive oil
1 large onion – chopped
1 bunch of spring onions – chopped (about 7/8 in total)
1 dessertspoon of fresh ginger – peeled and grated
1 red chilli – deseeded and chopped
1 teaspoon of dried chilli powder – optional
Raw shelled prawns – about 1 kg
2 heads of pak choi – chopped
1 tablespoon of teriyaki sauce
Handful of sesame seeds for garnish
Splash of water

Equipment

Wok or frying pan
Hob

■ *Tips and Tricks*

If you're serving rice – get it ready before you start cooking the prawns, and keep it warm in the oven.

What to Do

1. Heat the sesame oil in the wok and add the onions, the spring onions, grated ginger and chopped chilli and chilli powder, if you're using it, and cook for 3 or 4 minutes
2. Add the prawns, and cook for a few more minutes until they are pink and cooked through.
3. Add the chopped pak choi and teriyaki sauce and cook for a further minute or 2 with the lid on the wok – taking care not to overcook the pak choi. Add a splash of water and a bit more teriyaki sauce if you want more juice.

This is ready in minutes. You can swap the prawns for thinly sliced beef which is great with this combination of flavours too. Heat up a frying pan with a dash of olive oil and when it's sizzling, add the sliced steak and flash fry each side to brown the steak (for seconds if you like it rare), and keep it warm in a slow oven. Stir in the beef at the end after the pak choi. Allow a medium slice of steak each.

Serve with rice or egg noodles and garnish with sesame seeds.

Serves 4-6

SALMON PESTO

Ingredients

4 salmon fillets – skinned
1 tablespoon of pesto
1 tablespoon of tomato purée
12 sun-dried tomatoes – drained and chopped
Small tin of pitted black olives – drained
1 tablespoon of chopped thyme
10 cherry tomatoes
Sprinkle of olive oil
1 lemon – zest and juice
1 lemon for garnish

Equipment

Oven: 190°C, 170°C fan, Gas Mark 5
Oven-proof dish

■ Tips and Tricks

No tuna? Any 'meaty' fish such as halibut, monkfish or cod loin are just as good.

If you've got time, leave the salmon to soak up the flavours for at least an hour before you start cooking.

What to Do

1. Mix together the pesto, the tomato purée, the zest and juice of the lemon and the sun-dried tomatoes and spread on top of the salmon.
2. Top with the olives, cherry tomatoes and the thyme and sprinkle lightly with olive oil.
3. Cover loosely with foil and bake in the preheated oven for 15 minutes. Check that the fish is cooked through, and if not, return to the oven for a few more minutes.

Garnish with lemon quarters – and serve with rice noodles or rice.

Serves 4

SALADE NIÇOISE

Ingredients

   2 tins of tuna – drained
   4 eggs – hard boiled
   8/10 baby tomatoes – halved
   1 tin of anchovies – drained
   1 small tin of pitted black olives – drained
   1 bag of green beans
   1 lettuce or a bag of ready-washed salad
   1 lemon

Dressing

   3 tablespoons of olive oil
   1 teaspoon of runny honey
   2-3 teaspoons of Dijon mustard
   2 teaspoons of white wine vinegar or juice of ½ a lemon

■ Tips and Tricks

This is a brilliant 'store-cupboard staple' and if you need to bulk it out, add more eggs, tomatoes and cooked new potatoes.

Equipment

Hob
Can opener

What to Do

1. Cook the eggs in boiling water for about 10 minutes. Drain and cover with cold water and leave to cool before shelling.
2. Steam or boil the green beans for no more than a few minutes, drain and plunge into cold water.
3. Wash the lettuce, chop it up and put in a large salad bowl.
4. Take the beans out of the cold water and add to the salad.
5. Drain the tinned tuna, break up with a fork and pile on top of the salad.
6. Peel and quarter the eggs and arrange them on top with the drained anchovies, pitted olives and tomatoes.
7. Mix together the ingredients for the salad dressing in a jar with a lid, shake to combine and pour over the salad.

For the genuine version, do this with fresh tuna. Drizzle with olive oil and a squeeze of lemon juice – and sauté for a few minutes on each side. Break the cooked tuna up into chunks and pile it on top of the salad.

Serves 4

SALMON AND BLACK BEAN SAUCE

Ingredients

4 salmon fillets – with skin
1 tablespoon of olive oil
1 tablespoon of fresh ginger – grated
1 bunch of spring onions – topped, tailed and chopped
2 heads of pak choi, mange tout or broccoli
6 mushrooms – sliced
2 tablespoons of black bean sauce

Tips and Tricks

If you don't have black bean sauce – teriyaki sauce and a splash of soy sauce do just as well.

Equipment

Wok
Hob
Oven – on low heat

What to Do

1 Heat the oil in a wok or frying pan and fry the salmon, skin side down for about 4 minutes and then turn over and cook for a further 2 minutes. Check it's done by piercing the middle with a knife.
2 Cover and keep warm in a low oven.
3 Add a splash more of olive oil and fry the ginger, the chopped spring onions and the mushrooms for 2 minutes until they are beginning to soften.
4 Add the pak choi, mange tout or broccoli, toss in the black bean sauce and a splash of water and heat through for another minute or so until the vegetables are hot through – but still crispy.

Serve with rice.

Serves 4

SPICED COD

Ingredients

1 tablespoon of olive oil
4 medium cod loins – roughly cubed
1 tin of tomatoes
10 sun-dried tomatoes in oil – chopped and drained
1 tin of lentils
2 teaspoons of harissa paste
1 bunch of spring onions – chopped
Lemon wedges
Chopped parsley

Equipment

Frying pan or wok
Hob

■ *Tips and Tricks*

If you like 'spicy hot' – add another teaspoon or 2 of harissa paste – but taste and check before getting carried away.

What to Do

1 Heat the oil in a wok and add the chopped spring onions and fry for 2 or 3 minutes before adding the tinned tomatoes, the lentils, the harissa paste and the sun-dried tomatoes.
2 Heat to simmering point and then add the cod and simmer gently for a further 5 or 6 minutes, or until the fish is cooked and hot through.
3 Garnish with a lemon wedge and chopped parsley.

Just serve with a green salad.

Serves 4

PORK AND HAM

Barbequed Pork Kebabs
Gammon and Parsley Sauce
Paprika Pork
Patch's Pork
Pork Steaks with Caramelised Onions
Pork with Mushrooms, Onions and Garlic
Pork Steaks with Pak Choi
Toad in the Hole

BARBEQUED PORK KEBABS

Ingredients

1 fillet of pork – cut into cubes
8 small mushrooms
2 medium onions – cubed
Bunch of spring onions
2 cloves of garlic – crushed
1 tablespoon of fish sauce
2 tablespoons of teriyaki sauce
1 tablespoon of soy sauce
1 red chilli – diced
2 teaspoons of soft brown sugar
1 dessertspoon of grated ginger
2 limes (zest and juice of 1 – the other for garnish)
Handful of mint

Equipment

Skewers (if using wooden ones – soak for at least 30 minutes)
Barbeque or medium grill

■ Tips and Tricks

I love barbeques – but get it lit in plenty of time and make sure all the salads and sauces are prepared well in advance.

Metal skewers aren't expensive and so much better than the wooden ones which despite rumours to the contrary, I find they scorch and disintegrate.

What to Do

1. Crush the garlic, chop the spring onions, grate the ginger and put them in a bowl with the fish sauce, the teriyaki sauce, soy sauce, sugar, diced chilli, zest and juice of 1 lime and add 2/3 tablespoons of water.
2. Cut the pork fillet into 'bite-sized' chunks, and coat with the marinade for at least an hour – or better still, overnight.
3. Thread the pork, the mushrooms and onions onto the skewers and cook over the barbeque for about 10-15 minutes – turning frequently – and baste with the marinade.
4. Check the meat is cooked right through and not pink in the middle.

Give each person a skewer and garnish with the remaining lime, cut into quarters, scatter the chopped mint – and serve with coleslaw (page 176), tzatziki (page 224) and a warmed pita bread.

Ring the changes and use chicken breasts or boneless chicken thighs – just check it's cooked right through before serving.

This recipe also works brilliantly with beef – but it has to be a good cut, such as sirloin which is expensive but worth it for a treat. Instead of cubing the meat, marinade whole steaks as above, cut out the fish sauce and put in an extra tablespoon of teriyaki. Give it a few minutes each side to seal and seer the steak on a very hot barbeque. Cut into the steak and if it's too pink – return it to the barbeque for a few more minutes.

Serves 4

MIDDLE: PORK AND HAM

GAMMON AND PARSLEY SAUCE

Ingredients

1 medium joint of boned gammon (about 2 kg)
1 large orange – juice and zest
3 tablespoons of runny honey
2 dessertspoons of grainy mustard

Equipment

Hob
Large saucepan
Roasting tray
Small mixing bowl
Oven: 180°C, 160°C fan, Gas Mark 6

■ *Tips and Tricks*

This has got to have parsley sauce, in my view, (page 207), broad beans and jacket spuds with port and cranberry sauce on page 217 and a green veg. If you're short of time, just serve cranberry sauce without the port.

The cooking time can be tricky with this as it depends on how thick the joint is, but as a rough guide, 1½ hours in the oven with the foil on and another 10-15 minutes with the foil opened up should fit the bill.

What to Do

1. Cover the gammon joint in cold water, bring to simmering point and continue cooking gently for about 20 minutes. This just removes the excessive salty taste – without losing any of the flavour.
2. Take the gammon out of the water and if it has skin on, remove it carefully with a sharp knife and then secure the joint with string, so it keeps its shape during the next stage of cooking.
3. In a mixing bowl, combine the honey, mustard, orange juice and zest.
4. Line the roasting tin with foil and put the gammon joint in the foil, pour over the honey, mustard and orange juice and seal up the edges of the foil to make a tent.
5. Cook in the preheated oven for 1½ hours – basting once or twice during this time to keep the joint moist.
6. Open up the foil, baste and continue to cook for another 10-15 minutes until it is looking golden.
7. Dish the gammon onto a warmed serving dish and reserve the cooking juices.
8. Carve the gammon in thin slices and pour over the cooking juices.

I have only just discovered that gammon is the uncooked version, and once it is cooked, it becomes ham. You learn something every day.

Serves 6-8

PAPRIKA PORK

Ingredients

4 pork steaks
2 tablespoons of olive oil
1 lemon – zest and juice
Handful of thyme – chopped
1 large onion – peeled and chopped
2 tablespoons of paprika
1 tablespoon of tomato purée
1 teaspoon runny honey
3 mugs of vegetable stock
Tin of lentils – drained and rinsed
1 small green cabbage (shredded)

Equipment

Medium grill or BBQ
Hob

■ Tips and Tricks

Pork and cabbage is a classic combination, and this dish makes the best of both. If you want to cut down on the meat – substitute with extra lentils.

What to Do

1. Mix a tablespoon of olive oil with the lemon zest and juice and the thyme leaves, rub into the pork steaks and season with salt and pepper.
2. Heat the remaining oil in the pan, and add the peeled and chopped onion, and cook gently on the hob for 6 or 7 minutes until it is just beginning to soften.
3. Add the paprika, tomato purée, honey, stock and lentils, and simmer gently until hot through.
4. Cover and set aside.
5. Meanwhile, grill the pork steaks gently under a medium grill, or on a BBQ, until browned on both sides for at least 5 minutes each side depending on the thickness. Pierce with a knife and check the juices run clear, if they are still pink, return to the grill for a few minutes more.
6. Serve with the lentils.

I don't think this needs any extra carbs – just a green salad.

Serves 4

PATCH'S PORK

Ingredients

1 medium-sized boned loin of pork (about 1.5kg)
2 large cooking apples
2 large onions
1 medium bottle of dry cider
1 teaspoon of rock salt
2 tablespoons of olive oil

Equipment

Roasting tin
Oven: 220°C, 200°C fan, Gas Mark 7 (reducing after 20 minutes)

■ *Tips and Tricks*

If the crackling isn't crispy, slice it off carefully with a sharp knife and put it under a hot grill for a few minutes, skin side up – this normally does the trick. Keep your eye on it – it's easy to overdo it. Timing is hard with this pork as it depends on how thick the joint is. Roughly, it's 20 minutes on high, an hour on lower heat, and a further 20-30 minutes. Keep checking during the cooking time and add more cider if it needs it. Always check carefully that it is cooked through with clear juices when you pierce it.

What to Do

1. Take the pork out of the fridge an hour before cooking, pat the skin dry with kitchen roll and rub salt into the skin. After about 30 minutes, the skin will begin to sweat – pat it dry again and rub in more salt with a tablespoon of oil.
2. To start cooking, put the roasting tin in the preheated oven with a good splash of olive oil on the base.
3. Peel and roughly slice the apples and onions.
4. When the tin is good and hot, remove carefully from the oven and make a base of the apples and onions and put the pork joint on top. Sprinkle the remaining tablespoon of olive oil – and a bit more if you need it – over the apples and onions.
5. Return the tin to the oven, and roast for about 20 minutes on high heat before pouring in 2 big wine glasses of cider over the apples and onions in the base – but not over the pork.
6. Turn the oven down to 180°C, 160°C fan and Gas Mark 4.
7. Return to the tin to the oven for another hour.
8. Check the oven during this stage and pour in more cider if it looks as if it's getting too dry.
9. Put the tin back into the oven for a further 20-30 minutes.
10. Take the roasting tin out of the oven and pierce the pork with a skewer or knife, and if the juices are pink – put the pork back in the oven for another 10-15 minutes – and check again.
11. If the crackling is crisp and golden – and the joint looks 'done' – it probably is.
12. Take the pork out of the oven, cover in foil and a clean tea towel and leave to 'rest' while you get the veg ready.
13. Carve the pork and put a dollop of the apple and onion mixture on each plate – you won't need any extra gravy – and serve with roasted potatoes with rosemary and garlic (page 192) and a green veg such as broccoli.

This looks long-winded, with patting and checking and adding this and that – but it's delicious and worth a bit of extra trouble.

This was created by my son, Patch, when he was a student. He phoned one day and asked how to cook pork. I gave him the basic principles, but the apples, onions and cider were his idea – and to my mind, this is what cooking is about. There's no substitute for a bit of experimenting. You don't always get it right, but have a go.

Serves 6-8

PORK STEAKS WITH CARAMELISED ONIONS

Ingredients

4 pork steaks
12 shallots or baby onions
1 tablespoon of flour
2 tablespoons of sherry or white wine
1 mug of vegetable stock
1 teaspoon of brown sugar
2 dessertspoons of balsamic vinegar
Scoop of butter
2 tablespoons of olive oil

Equipment

Wok or frying pan
Hob
Warm oven

Tips and Tricks

The sticky shallots go really well with the pork, and the splash or sherry adds depth to the sauce. If you don't have sherry in stock – wine does just as well.

What to Do

1. Put the shallots in a heatproof dish and pour over boiling water and leave to stand for 2 or 3 minutes. (This makes them much easier to peel.) Remove them carefully from the water and peel and chop them.
2. Heat the butter and a splash of the olive oil in a pan, gently cook the shallots for about 10 minutes before adding the balsamic vinegar and teaspoon of brown sugar. Continue cooking and shaking the pan for a further 4 or 5 minutes until the onions are looking caramelised and slightly sticky.
3. Remove from the pan, cover and put into a heatproof dish in a low oven.
4. Add another splash of olive oil to the pan and when sizzling, add the pork steaks, turn the heat down a bit and cook for 5/6 minutes each side, or until they are cooked through and the juices run clear when you pierce them.
5. Remove the pork steaks from the pan when they are ready and put them in the low oven.
6. Reserve the cooking juices and add the flour to the pan off the heat, stir in the sherry (or wine if you prefer), stock and shallots, simmer for 5 minutes until thickened and then pour over the pork steaks.

Serve with mashed spud and a green veg such as broccoli or frozen peas.

Serves 4

PORK WITH MUSHROOMS, ONIONS AND GARLIC

Ingredients

4 pork steaks, trimmed of fat
2 tablespoons of olive oil
2 cloves of garlic – crushed
8 medium-sized mushrooms
1 large onion – chopped
1 teaspoon of Dijon mustard
1 dessertspoon of flour
1 small glass of white wine
1 tablespoon of chopped tarragon or thyme
1 tablespoon of single cream or natural yoghurt

Equipment

Wok or frying pan
Oven-proof dish
Warm oven

■ Tips and Tricks

If you want to cut down on calories, swap the cream for yoghurt, but add it at the last stage when you stir in the herbs and heat very gently.

What to Do

1. Heat the oil in a wok, add the pork steaks and sauté on a medium heat for about 5 minutes each side until just turning brown. Check the juices run clear.
2. Remove from the pan, cover and keep warm in the oven.
3. Put an extra splash of oil in the pan, and when just sizzling, add the chopped onions and crushed garlic and cook for about 5 minutes, until just beginning to soften.
4. Take off the heat and stir in the flour to combine the cooking juices, return to the heat and add the mustard, chopped mushrooms, cream and wine, and simmer for a few minutes until the sauce is just thickening.
5. Put the pork into the sauce and heat through for a further 5 minutes and check that it's hot through.
6. Add the chopped tarragon or thyme.
7. Serve with hot, buttered noodles and a green salad.

Serves 4

PORK STEAKS WITH PAK CHOI

Ingredients

4 pork steaks
Small red chilli – seeded and finely chopped
2 tablespoons of soy sauce
1 clove of garlic – crushed
1 dessertspoon of balsamic vinegar
1 tablespoon of sesame oil
1 tablespoon of olive oil
Handful of sesame seeds
2 heads of pak choi – or cabbage (finely chopped)
1 tablespoon of sesame seeds (optional)

Equipment

Low oven
Frying pan or wok
Hob

■ Tips and Tricks

Green cabbage works just as well with this –or any green vegetable such as broccoli or green beans.

What to Do

1. Mix together garlic, chillies, sesame oil, balsamic vinegar and soy sauce, pour over the pork and leave to marinade for at least an hour or overnight in the fridge if you have time.
2. Heat the olive oil in the wok until it's sizzling.
3. Remove the pork from the marinade and reserve it.
4. Sauté the pork both sides for about 5 minute each side, depending on the thickness of the steaks.
5. Pierce the pork with a knife and if the juices are clear, transfer to a heatproof serving dish in a low oven. If the juices are pink, continue cooking for another few minutes.
6. Meanwhile, return the wok with the reserved juices to the hob and bring to simmering point and continue cooking for a minute or 2.
7. Add the pak choi and heat through until it's just wilting.
8. Take the pork out of the oven, add in the pak choi and juices on top, sprinkle with sesame seeds and serve.

All this needs is rice.

Serves 4

TOAD IN THE HOLE

Ingredients

8/10 best quality sausages
1 medium onion
1 heaped tablespoon of plain flour
2 eggs
1 mug of milk
1 tablespoon of chopped thyme (optional)
1 dessertspoon of olive oil

Equipment

Oven: 220°C, 200°C fan or Gas Mark 7
Electric whisk
Large roasting tin

■ Tips and Tricks

I have to admit to being a sausage snob – there's nothing to beat proper sausages from the butcher – it makes all the difference. If you're getting them from the supermarket, get top of the range.

What to Do

1. Put the sausages, chopped onions and chopped thyme in the roasting tin in the preheated oven and drizzle with olive oil.
2. Bake for about 15 minutes or until the sausages and onions are just beginning to turn at the edges.
3. While the sausages are in the oven, mix the flour, milk and eggs in a bowl and beat to a smooth mixture and season to taste.
4. Take the roasting tin out of the oven and immediately pour the batter over the sausages while the pan is sizzling.
5. Return to the oven for about 30 or 40 minutes until the batter is crisp and well risen.

Just like mum did it – good, old fashioned, comforting toad in the hole. If you really want a treat, serve it with onion gravy (page 216) – and tomato ketchup is a must.

Serves 4

Brochettes of Lamb
Butterflied Lamb
Greek Lamb Skewers
Harissa Lamb
Jen's Leg of Lamb
Lamb Korma
Mince
Moussaka
Spicy Marinated Lamb

BROCHETTES OF LAMB WITH PESTO

Ingredients

4-5 lamb steaks – cut into cubes
1 tablespoon of olive oil
2 cloves of garlic – crushed
1 lemon – juice and zest
2/3 sprigs of rosemary

For the Pesto

Bunch of basil leaves
Bunch of fresh mint
1 heaped tablespoon of Parmesan cheese
2 tablespoons of pine nuts
1 clove of garlic
Juice of half a lemon
2 tablespoons of olive oil

Equipment

Grill or Barbeque
Skewers – metal or wooden
Blender

Tips and Tricks

If you're using wooden skewers, soak them for a few hours in water to prevent them from burning.

If you don't have time to prepare the pesto, just use the ready-made version from a jar.

What to Do

1. Combine the olive oil, garlic, lemon juice and zest in a bowl, and cut the lamb into bite-sized cubes.
2. Coat the lamb with the oil mixture and, if you have time, refrigerate for an hour or 2 before you're ready to start cooking.
3. To prepare the pesto, whizz all the ingredients in the blender and season to taste, put the mixture into a bowl and refrigerate.
4. In the meantime, thread the lamb on to skewers (preferably metal ones) and put into a preheated hot grill or barbeque, and cook for about 8 minutes for pink lamb or longer if you like it well done.
5. Keep turning the lamb so it cooks evenly.

Serve immediately, with the pesto, a green salad and warmed pita bread.

Serves 4

BUTTERFLIED LAMB

Ingredients

1 leg of lamb – butterflied (about 1.5-2 kg)
4 large garlic cloves – crushed
3 lemons – zest of 1 – juice of 3
2 tablespoons of ras el hanout
5 tablespoons of olive oil
1 dessertspoon of runny honey

Equipment

Roasting tray
Oven: 220°C, 200°C fan and Gas Mark 7

■ *Tips and Tricks*

Ras el hanout is a Moroccan spice mix that you can find on most supermarket shelves.

It's worth asking your butcher to 'butterfly' the lamb for you. Failing that, sometimes you can find lamb already butterflied in the supermarket.

What to Do

1. Mix together the ras el hanout with the olive oil, garlic, lemon juice and zest and the runny honey and smear over the lamb.
2. If you have time, put it into a non-metallic dish to marinade, cover and refrigerate overnight.
3. If you're short of time, cook it straight away.
4. Put the lamb into the preheated oven in a roasting tin, with an extra glug of olive oil and roast for 15 minutes on high heat and then turn down to 180°C, 160 fan and Gas Mark 4, and continue cooking for another 30 minutes.
5. Put a skewer into the thickest part of the lamb and if it's too pink, return it for another 10 or 15 minutes.
6. Serve the lamb onto a warmed dish, cover with foil and a clean tea towel and leave to rest for about 15 minutes.

This goes perfectly with Honey and Lemon Couscous on page 177, tzatziki on page 224 and redcurrant jelly.

Serves 6-8

GREEK LAMB SKEWERS

Ingredients

Lamb mince – about 500g
2 tablespoons of chopped oregano or thyme
1 lemon – juice and zest
1 dessertspoon of flour
1 egg – beaten
Handful of mint for garnish

Equipment

Grill or BBQ
Skewers

■ *Tips and Tricks*

If you want a spicier flavour, add a teaspoon each of ground coriander and cumin and a finely chopped chilli.

What to Do

1 Preheat the grill or light the barbeque.
2 Combine the mince with the oregano, lemon juice and zest, flour and beaten egg.
3 Divide the mixture into 8 equal parts and then squeeze around the skewers.
4 Keep refrigerated for at least an hour before you start cooking.
5 Grill the skewers for about 10 minutes – turning a few times so they don't overdo – but are browned evenly.

Serve with warmed pita bread and tzatziki on page 224, and garnish with mint.

Serves 4-6

HARISSA LAMB

Ingredients

Medium leg of lamb – on the bone (about 1.5 kg)
3 tablespoons of olive oil
4 garlic cloves
2 dessertspoons of fresh ginger – grated
2 large glasses of dry sherry (optional)
2 tablespoons of soy sauce
1 heaped dessertspoon of soft brown sugar
6 tablespoons of teriyaki sauce
3 teaspoons of harissa paste
1 medium chilli – deseeded and diced (optional)
Juice and zest of an orange
Zest of lemon and a squeeze of juice
2 heads of broccoli
Bunch of spring onions – chopped
Egg noodles (125 g)

Equipment

Roasting tin
Oven: 200°C, 180°C fan and Gas Mark 6

▌*Tips and Tricks*

Experiment with this; add more harissa and more chilli if you like it hotter.

Fresh noodles definitely work best, but if you can't get them, use the dried variety – but factor in the extra cooking time.

I like lamb pink, but if you prefer it well done, add another 20 minutes to the cooking time below. Put a skewer into it and if it's still pink – put it back for a bit longer.

What to Do

1. Preheat the oven and put a good splash of olive oil in the roasting tin. When it's sizzling add the lamb and roast for 15 minutes, or until the skin is just turning brown.
2. While the lamb is in the oven, peel and grate the ginger and crush the garlic and mix together in a bowl with the sherry, brown sugar, teriyaki sauce, soy sauce, chilli, orange juice and zest, lemon juice and zest and 3 mugs of water.
3. Take the lamb out of the oven after 15 minutes, and set aside while you line the roasting tin with 2 layers of foil, crossed over, return the lamb to the tin and tip the teriyaki mixture over the lamb.
4. Seal up the foil to form a tent.
5. Reduce the oven to 180°C, 160°C fan, Gas Mark 4, and return the lamb to the oven for an hour.
6. Open out the foil and add a bit more water and another splash of teriyaki sauce if it looks as if it's getting too dry and baste the lamb with the mixture.
7. Roast the lamb for another 15-20 minutes with the foil opened out for pink, or an additional 30 minutes if you like it well done.
8. Dish up the lamb into a warmed serving dish, cover with foil and a clean tea towel and leave it to rest.
9. Tip the cooking juices from the foil back into the roasting pan and heat gently on the hob and add another splash of sherry, soy sauce and teriyaki if it needs bulking out.
10. Add the spring onions and the broccoli and simmer for a few minutes.
11. Meanwhile, cook and drain the noodles – which only take a few minutes – and add them to the veg.
12. Carve the lamb and serve the noodles, veg and lamb straight on to warmed plates.

If you feel you need more veg steam some extra broccoli.

Serves 6

JEN'S ROAST LAMB

Ingredients

1 leg of lamb on the bone (about 1.5 kg)
5 cloves of garlic
4 sprigs of fresh rosemary
2 tablespoons of olive oil
4 tablespoons of redcurrant jelly
3 tablespoons of red wine vinegar
1 bunch of fresh mint

Equipment

Oven: 220°C, 200°C fan, Gas Mark 7
Roasting tin
Hob

■ *Tips and Tricks*

A medium-size leg of lamb will be quite pink after 1½ hours so add some extra time if you prefer it better done.

What to Do

1. Make 6 or 7 incisions in the lamb with a sharp knife and put some rosemary leaves and garlic into the gap, and rub olive oil and salt over the skin.
2. Line the roasting tin with 2 sheets of foil, crossed over and when the oven is hot, put the lamb into the foil and seal it up loosely and put it into the oven.
3. Roast for 30 minutes on high temperature and then reduce the oven to 200°C, 180°C fan and Gas Mark 6, and continue cooking for another 30 minutes.
4. While the lamb is roasting, put the redcurrant jelly, chopped mint and vinegar into a saucepan and heat gently until the jelly has melted and set aside.
5. Take the lamb out of the oven and spread a tablespoon of the redcurrant mixture on the lamb. Open up the foil and continue roasting for a further 30 minutes so the skin has browned nicely.
6. Remove the lamb from the oven and cut into the meat in the centre of the joint to check if it is done enough.
7. If you're happy, put it on to a warmed serving dish, cover with foil and a clean tea towel, and allow to rest for 15 minutes.
8. Return the redcurrant mixture to the hob and heat gently.
9. In a separate pan, add the cooking juices and simmer for a minute or 2, until it's piping hot.
10. Transfer the cooking juices to a jug, carve the lamb and pour sparingly over each helping.
11. Serve the redcurrant sauce separately.

This is a recipe of my sister, Jen's. She always says lamb needs either to be served pink, or cooked until it falls off the bone. Jen's Roast Lamb is best pink, we think. But the choice is yours.

Garlic and rosemary potatoes on page 192 and mushy peas on page 182 go brilliantly with this.

Serves 6-8

LAMB KORMA

Ingredients

4-5 lamb steaks
1 tablespoon of olive oil
2 medium onions, peeled and chopped
2 cloves of garlic, crushed
2 dessertspoons of fresh ginger – peeled and grated
2/3 teaspoons of cumin
1 teaspoon of turmeric
2 teaspoons of ground coriander
½ teaspoon of hot chilli powder
2 tablespoons of cashews
Small pot of natural yoghurt
Splash of single cream
Small bunch of coriander
Small bag of spinach

Equipment

Large saucepan
Hob

■ Tips and Tricks

If you want to plan ahead, cook the day before, cool and refrigerate overnight. Take the lamb out of the fridge and heat through gently on the hob to simmering point, add the cashews and after 10 minutes, add the yoghurt, cream, fresh coriander and spinach – until it's just wilting.

What to Do

1. Dice the lamb, peel and chop the onions, grate the garlic and peel and grate the fresh ginger.
2. Heat the olive oil in the wok and when it's sizzling, add the chopped onions and fry them on a high heat for 4 or 5 minutes until they are just beginning to soften, stirring continuously.
3. Keeping the heat high, chuck in the lamb and the garlic and continue cooking and stirring until it's just turning brown.
4. Stir in the cumin, turmeric, chilli powder and ground coriander.
5. Turn down the heat and add a mug of water.
6. Bring back slowly to simmering point, cover with a lid and cook gently for about 20 minutes.
7. Check that there's enough liquid – don't let the juices reduce, and at this point, add the cashew nuts – and then simmer for another 10 minutes.
8. Check for seasoning – and add a bit of salt if you think it needs it.
9. Add the small pot of yoghurt and heat through, but don't let it boil. Stir in a tiny splash of cream, and then add the chopped coriander and spinach until just wilting.

For the full works, serve with naan bread, rice, homemade tomato and onion relish (page 218) and mango chutney.

If you feel it needs cooling down, serve with tzatziki on page 224, but add ½ teaspoon of cumin to make it more Indian and less Greek.

If you're short of time – just go for rice.

Serves 4-6

LAMB MINCE

Ingredients

500 g of lamb mince
1 tablespoon of olive oil
2 large onions
1 tin of tomatoes
1 tablespoon of tomato purée or sun-dried tomato paste
1 mug of vegetable stock
Handful of fresh herbs – thyme or oregano
Glass of red wine
½ teaspoon of sugar

Equipment

Wok or deep frying pan
Hob

■ *Tips and Tricks*

You can top this with mashed spud for a shepherd's pie, or layer with aubergines and top with cheese sauce to make Moussaka on page 114.

What to Do

1. Peel and slice the onions and heat up the olive oil in the pan.
2. Throw the onions in the pan when it's sizzling, and cook on a high heat for about 5 minutes.
3. Put the mince into the pan and keep stirring for another 5 minutes until the lamb is turning brown.
4. Then add the remaining ingredients; the tomatoes, tomato purée or sundried tomato paste, vegetable stock, sugar, wine and herbs.
5. Check for taste – and add salt, pepper and a bit more tomato purée or sun-dried tomato paste if it needs more flavour.
6. Continue cooking for another 15-20 minutes.

Serves 4-6

MOUSSAKA

Ingredients

1 quantity of cooked lamb mince (page 112)
3 large aubergines – sliced
2-3 tablespoons of olive oil

Topping

Large carton of natural yoghurt
1 large egg – beaten
1 heaped tablespoon of Parmesan cheese
½ a pack of feta cheese

Equipment

Large oven-proof dish – about 25cm square
Frying pan
Electric whisk
Oven: 180°C, 160°C fan, Gas Mark 4
Medium grill
Hob

▇ Tips and Tricks

You can top this with cheese sauce on page 206, but I find the yoghurt and feta more 'authentic Greek'.

What to Do

1 Slice the aubergines and sprinkle with salt to allow them to 'sweat' for about 15 minutes and then dab with kitchen roll.
2 Coat the aubergines both sides with olive oil and put under the preheated grill for about 4 or 5 minutes each side, until they are just beginning to tinge.
3 Put half of the mince in the oven-proof dish and cover with half of the aubergines.
4 Repeat with the remainder of the mince and aubergines.
5 Beat the yoghurt, egg and half of the Parmesan with the electric mixer and pour onto the mince and aubergines.
6 Crumble the feta cheese and sprinkle onto the topping with the remainder of the Parmesan.
7 Bake in the preheated oven for 30-40 minutes until it's golden brown.

This can be made the day before, just cool and refrigerate and heat up for 30 minutes as above.

All this needs is a green salad.

Serves 4-6

Beef Goulash
Beef Stroganoff
Boeuf Bourguignon
Cottage Pie
Chilli Beef
Chilli Con Carne
Dee's Cumberland Pie
Lasagne
Meatballs
Mince
Tom's Chilli Burgers

BEEF GOULASH

Ingredients

4 slices of braising steak (about a kg) – cut into thin strips
2 tablespoons of olive oil
1 heaped tablespoon of flour
8 slices of streaky bacon
2 medium onions – peeled and sliced
2 cloves of garlic
4 tablespoons of paprika
2 sachets of bouquet garni
1 can of chopped tomatoes
1 tablespoon of tomato purée
2 mugs of beef stock
2 tablespoons of soured cream

Equipment

Flameproof casserole dish
Hob
Oven: 170°C, 150°C fan, Gas Mark 3

■ Tips and Tricks

This Hungarian casserole, traditionally flavoured with paprika, combined with the soured cream, gives a rich but not overpowering flavour. Unlike its cousin, Beef Stroganoff (page 120) – which is cooked in minutes – this benefits from long, slow cooking.

You can prepare this the day before – but don't add the soured cream until just before serving.

What to Do

1. Cut the beef into thin slices and coat with the flour.
2. Heat 1 tablespoon of olive oil in a flameproof casserole dish and gently fry the onions and bacon for about 5 minutes, add the garlic, cook for a further minute or 2 and then transfer to a bowl or plate.
3. Put the remaining oil in the flameproof casserole dish, and when sizzling, fry the beef in batches – for a minute or 2 – until it is beginning to brown.
4. Return the onions, bacon and garlic to the dish with the beef and add the bouquet garni, beef stock, tomatoes, tomato purée and paprika, and simmer gently in a low oven for between 1½-2 hours.
5. Keep your eye on it to check it isn't getting dry. Add another splash of stock, if necessary.
6. Just before serving, swirl in the soured cream.

All it needs is noodles and a green salad.

Serves 4

BEEF STROGANOFF

Ingredients

4 slices of sirloin steak or fillet
1 tablespoon of paprika
2 tablespoons of olive oil
1 tablespoon of butter
2 medium onions – peeled and sliced
6 medium button mushrooms – sliced
½ lemon, squeezed
2 tablespoons of soured cream
Scoop of butter
Small handful of parsley

Equipment

Heavy-bottomed frying pan
Ovenproof dish for serving
Hob

■ Tips and Tricks

Timing is critical with this dish. Make sure the noodles are cooked, add a cube of butter to them, cover and keep warm in a low oven before you prepare the onions, mushrooms and steak – so you're ready to serve as soon as the steak is done.

What to Do

1. Slice the meat into strips about 2-3 cm thick, season with salt and pepper and set aside.
2. Heat up a tablespoon of olive oil in a heavy-bottomed frying pan, add the sliced onions and sauté for about 5 minutes – or until they are softened.
3. Add the mushrooms to the pan with the onions, cook for a further 2/3 minutes and add a squeeze of lemon.
4. Lift the pan off the heat and stir in the soured cream and paprika into the onion and mushroom mixture, and put it back onto the hob to heat gently for 2 or 3 minutes, until the cream is combined and the mushrooms are softened.
5. Put the onions and mushrooms into a warmed ovenproof dish in a low oven while you prepare the steak.
6. Wipe the pan clean with kitchen roll and add the other tablespoon of olive oil and the butter and when it's sizzling hot, add the steak and seer quickly to seal it – for no more than 30 seconds each side, if you like steak rare – or a bit longer, if not.
7. Add the steak, with the cooking juices, to the onion and mushroom mix – and taste for seasoning.
8. Beef Stroganoff is closely related to Beef Goulash; the difference being the length of time to cook and the different cut of meat.
9. Serve with rice and a salad.

Serves 4

BOEUF BOURGUIGNON

Ingredients

1 kg of topside or rump steak
Generous chunk of butter (about ¼ pack)
3-4 tablespoons of olive oil
2 cloves of garlic
2 medium onions – peeled and chopped
10 slices of streaky bacon – sliced
2 tablespoons of flour
½ tin of consommé soup
1 heaped tablespoon of tomato purée
2/3 glasses of red wine
16 baby onions – peeled and left whole
16 button mushrooms
Bouquet garni or a handful of fresh herbs – thyme or sage

Equipment

Casserole dish with lid
Frying pan/wok
Hob
Oven: 170°C, 150°C fan, Gas Mark 3

■ *Tips and Tricks*

This classic French dish simmers slowly in wine and herbs until it's almost falling apart. If you get the chance, make this a day ahead and stick it in the fridge – it definitely improves the flavour. It will just need heating gently on the hob or reheating in the oven for about 30 minutes on 180°C, 160°C fan or Gas Mark 4.

Go easy on the wine – I think too much wine can give the meat a bitter taste – but the combination of wine and consommé works best.

What to Do

1. Peel and slice the onions and cut the meat into cubes.
2. Heat 1 tablespoon of olive oil and the butter in a casserole dish on the hob and lob in the chopped onions, the sliced bacon and the garlic, and fry for about 6 or 7 minutes, stirring frequently, until just turning golden. Remove from the pan and set aside.
3. Wipe clean the casserole dish with kitchen roll, heat up another tablespoon of oil, add the cubed beef to the casserole dish and seer it for about 5 or 6 minutes – stirring continuously to seal the meat.
4. Return the onions and bacon to the pan with the meat, take it off the heat and stir in the flour.
5. When it's combined, chuck in the consommé soup, the wine, the tomato purée and the bouquet garni, and bring gently to simmering point on the hob.
6. Put the lid on the casserole dish and put it into the preheated oven and cook for at least 2½-3 hours. Check 2 or 3 times, give it a stir and make sure it's not getting too dry, and if it is, add a bit more consommé and a splash more wine and water.
7. While the casserole is in the oven – prepare the baby onions.
8. Put them in a heatproof dish and cover with boiling water for 2 or 3 minutes. Take them out of the hot water carefully and take off the tops, tails and skins and leave them whole.
9. Heat up another tablespoon of olive oil in a frying pan – and fry gently for about 6 minutes, shaking the pan – so they brown evenly.
10. Give the whole mushrooms the same treatment.
11. Put the baby onions in the casserole an hour before the end of the cooking time –and the mushrooms half an hour before the end of the cooking time.

The tomato purée in this dish just adds a bit of richness – and if you can't find consommé soup – just use a mug or 2 of beef stock.

This is best with mashed spud and a green veg, such as steamed broccoli – or peas and rice, if you run out of time.

Serves 6-8

COTTAGE PIE

Ingredients

1 quantity of basic Beef Mince (page 138)
4-5 large potatoes – peeled and chopped
Splash of milk
¼ pack of butter
1 tablespoon of Parmesan

Equipment

Large saucepan
Hob
Ovenproof dish
Oven: 200°C, 180°C fan, Gas Mark 6

■ *Tips and Tricks*

This is a good alternative to spaghetti. Leave out the Parmesan if you want a less rich flavour.

What to do for the Topping

1. Peel and roughly cut the potatoes.
2. Boil for about 15 minutes until they are soft.
3. Drain and mash them with the milk and butter until there are no lumps.
4. Fork evenly on top of the mince making sure you spread it up to the edges of the dish to seal it.
5. Sprinkle with the Parmesan.
6. Bake in the preheated oven for about 30-40 minutes until the top just begins to turn golden – and bubbling.

Serve with frozen peas and tomato ketchup – job done.

Serves 4-6

CHILLI BEEF

Ingredients

    4 slices of sirloin steak – cut into strips
    1 dessertspoon of sesame oil
    1 tablespoon of olive oil
    1 tablespoon of soy sauce
    4 tablespoons of black bean sauce
    2 cloves of garlic
    1 dessertspoon of grated ginger
    Large bunch of spring onions
    2 cloves of garlic – crushed
    1 medium red chilli – seeded and chopped
    Handful of mange tout
    1 broccoli head – chopped
    1 red pepper – deseeded and cut into strips
    1-2 teaspoons of honey – optional

Equipment

Wok
Hob
Oven

■ *Tips and Tricks*

This sticky beef stir fry includes plenty of veg – and if you like it hotter – add a teaspoon of chilli flakes – but with caution. If you don't want to do a salad – just increase the amount of veg.

What to Do

1. Slice the beef into 2 or 3 cm strips.
2. Mix the sesame oil, soy sauce, garlic, chilli, ginger, black bean sauce and a splash of water.
3. Pour it over the steak and make sure it is coated evenly.
4. Leave to marinade in the fridge for 2 hours – or preferably overnight.
5. Cook the noodles and dish up into an ovenproof serving dish, cover and keep warm in the oven before starting to cook the beef – as it takes only a matter of minutes.
6. Remove the beef from the marinade and reserve the residue. Heat half the olive oil in a frying pan or wok until sizzling hot. Flash fry the beef for a minute each side – or less if you like it pink like I do – and then add it to the noodles in the oven.
7. Wipe the wok with kitchen roll to remove the meat residue and then heat up the remaining oil before adding the veg: the mange tout, broccoli, chopped spring onions and red pepper – and cook on a high heat for 3 or 4 minutes.
8. Return the beef strips to the pan – pour in the reserved marinade, heat through and serve immediately.

This is one of my favourites – and marinating the beef the day before tenderizes it – love it.

Serves 4

CHILLI CON CARNE

Ingredients

500 g of mince
2 tablespoons of olive oil
2 onions – chopped
2 cloves of garlic – crushed
1 tablespoon of tomato purée
1 teaspoon of chilli powder
1 teaspoon of chilli flakes
2 teaspoons of cumin
2 teaspoons of ground coriander
2 or 3 tablespoons of tomato passata
Splash of Worcestershire sauce
1 tin of chopped tomatoes
1 glass of red wine
2 tins of kidney beans
Pinch of sugar
1 mug of beef stock

Equipment

Large saucepan
Hob

■ *Tips and Tricks*

If you decide it needs more poke – add with caution, another half a teaspoon of chilli powder or extra cumin and coriander – and check for salt and pepper.

If you want to make this go further – put in an extra tin or two of kidney beans to the mince.

What to Do

1. Heat the oil in a large saucepan and add the chopped onions when it's good and hot. Cook for 3 or 4 minutes – stirring to stop it scorching and sticking to the pan.
2. Add the mince to the pan and cook over a high heat until it's beginning to brown – and keep stirring.
3. Stir the spices and crushed garlic into the onion and mince along with the tin of tomatoes, tomato purée, tomato passata and drained kidney beans.
4. Add the red wine, Worcestershire sauce and the beef stock and cook gently on the hob for about 30 minutes.

If you're feeding a crowd, simply double or triple the ingredients and dig out your biggest pan. All you need is hot plates and a few willing helpers to dole out – and big bowls of soured cream, grated cheese, boil in the bag rice and guacamole on page 208.

Serves 6-8

DEE'S CUMBERLAND PIE

Ingredients

Stewing steak – about 1 kg – cut into cubes
2 celery sticks – chopped
2 large onions – peeled and sliced
2 huge carrots – peeled and sliced
2-3 tablespoons of olive oil
2 tablespoons of flour
2 tablespoons of tomato purée
1 tablespoon of Worcestershire sauce
2 mugs of beef stock
Handful of herbs – thyme or oregano
4 or 5 large potatoes – peeled and sliced
1 tablespoon of grated Parmesan
1 tablespoon of Cheddar cheese

Equipment

Hob
Oven: 160°C, 140°C fan, Gas Mark 3
Flameproof pan with lid

■ Tips and Tricks

This can be made the day before. Put the spuds on top of the beef, cover and refrigerate when it's cool. Heat up in a preheated oven at 200°, 180°C fan, Gas Mark 6 for at least 30 minutes. Make sure it's piping hot before serving.

What to Do

1. Heat the oil in the flameproof pan on the hob and when it's sizzling, add the chopped celery sticks, the onions and carrots and cook for about 8 minutes, until the vegetables are softening.
2. Add the cubed beef and cook for another 5 minutes.
3. Take the pan off the heat and stir in the flour, the tomato purée, Worcestershire sauce, stock and herbs.
4. Return the pan to the heat, bring it gently to simmering point – and add a splash of water if it looks too thick.
5. Put the lid on the pan and transfer it to the preheated oven and cook for at least 2-2½ hours until the meat is really tender. Keep checking that it is not getting too dry and add a bit more stock if it needs it. If it's not tender – put it back for another 30 minutes.
6. Meanwhile, peel and halve the potatoes and boil them for about 8 minutes, until they are almost done but still 'crispy'. Drain them and slice them into roughly 2 cm slices.
7. Layer the potatoes on top of the beef – and sprinkle the grated Parmesan and Cheddar on top.
8. Return the dish to the oven without the lid – and turn it up to 200°C, 180°C fan, Gas Mark 6, and cook for a further 30 minutes until the potatoes are golden brown and crispy.

My good friend Dee cooked this for us – and she gave me the recipe – it is delicious. The addition of carrots and celery – and no red wine – somehow makes it slightly 'sweeter' than Boeuf Bourguignon.

Serves 8

LASAGNE

Ingredients

1 quantity of Basic Beef Mince (page 138)
1 pack of fresh lasagne sheets
Cheese sauce – double quantity (page 206)
2 tablespoons of Parmesan for sprinkling

Equipment

Oven 200, 180, Gas 5
Ovenproof dish – approximately 20cms x 25cms

■ *Tips and Tricks*

As with Chilli Con Carne – this is great for a crowd. You can prepare it the day before – and just shove it in the oven for 40 minutes until it's good and hot. If you have doubled or trebled the quantities and have two or three dishes – remember it will take longer to re-heat.

What to do

1. Prepare the Basic Beef Mince from page 138 and the Cheese Sauce from page 206.
2. Ladle half the mince into the ovenproof dish, top with lasagne sheets, then another layer of mince and another layer of lasagne.
3. Pour the Cheese Sauce on top, ensuring all the lasagne is covered.
4. Bake in the oven for 30 minutes until the top is just turning brown and the mixture is bubbling.
5. Ten minutes before serving, take the dish out of the oven, sprinkle two tablespoons of grated Parmesan on the top and return it to the oven for a further ten minutes.

Serve with a big bowl of green salad and garlic bread.

Serves 4-6

MEATBALLS

Ingredients for Tomato Sauce

2 onions – peeled and chopped
2 cloves of garlic – crushed
1 scoop of butter
1 tablespoon of olive oil
½ bottle of tomato passata
1 teaspoon of sugar
Cup of milk

Ingredients for Meatballs

500 g mince
2 tablespoons of breadcrumbs
1 beaten egg
Handful of chopped herbs
1 dessertspoon of flour

Equipment

Hob
Large saucepan

■ Tips and Tricks

If you're in a hurry, just grab a pack of ready-made meatballs from the supermarket, but if you've got a bit of time on your hands – you can make them yourself. Allow 4 medium meat balls or 6 small ones per head with the ready-made variety.

What to do – the Sauce

1. Heat the oil and butter in a pan and add the finely chopped onions and crushed garlic, and cook over a medium heat for 8 minutes until they are just softening.
2. Add the passata, milk and sugar, season to taste and bring gently to simmering point. Continue cooking for another 10 minutes.
3. Drop the meatballs in, one by one into the pan – being careful not to break them up.
4. Cover and simmer gently for about 20 minutes until the meatballs are brown, hot and cooked through.
5. Serve with plain noodles.

What to do – the Meatballs

1. Mix all the ingredients together in a large bowl and shape them into balls – roughly the size of a golf ball. They hold their shape better if you refrigerate them for an hour or 2 before cooking – or overnight.

Make them yourself – and you know exactly what's gone into them.

Serves 4-6 (4/5 meatballs per person)

MIDDLE: BEEF

MINCE

Ingredients

500 g of beef mince
2 tablespoons of olive oil
2 cloves of garlic – crushed
2 large onions – peeled and chopped
8/10 rashers or streaky bacon
1 tin of tomatoes
1 tablespoon of tomato purée
1 dessertspoon of sun-dried tomato paste
1 mug of tomato passata
1 mug of vegetable or beef stock
Pinch of sugar

Equipment

Large saucepan
Hob

■ Tips and Tricks

Good old mince! You can chuck it over pasta, make cottage pie on page 126 or lasagne on page 134 or dress it up as chilli con carne.

What to Do

1. Peel and slice the onions and dice the bacon.
2. Heat up the olive oil in the pan and when it's sizzling, add the onions, garlic and bacon and cook on a high heat for about 5 or 6 minutes.
3. Add the mince and continue cooking for a further 5 or 6 minutes until it is no longer pink.
4. Then add the remaining ingredients: the tinned tomatoes, tomato purée, sun-dried tomato paste, beef stock, a pinch of sugar and the tomato passata.
5. Continue cooking gently for another 15/20 minutes.

Serves 4

TOM'S CHILLI BURGERS

Ingredients

500 g of mince
1 tablespoon of olive oil
1 large onion, peeled and chopped
Handful of herbs – thyme or oregano
1 egg – beaten
1 tablespoon of flour
1 teaspoon of chilli flakes
Hamburger buns

Equipment

Hob
Frying pan
Barbeque

■ Tips and Tricks

These are best on a really hot barbeque. I like them cooked for 3 or 4 minutes each side – depending on the thickness of the burgers, so they are piping hot and golden on the outside but still pink in the middle. Cut into the middle of one burger to test it. If you like them less pink – leave them on for a bit longer – but turn frequently or they will overcook.

Timing with barbeques is crucial – so make sure you have all the extras at the ready; buns cut up, and salads prepared before you start cooking.

What to Do

1. Peel and finely chop the onion and sauté on a high heat on the hob for 5 minutes and set aside to cool.
2. Mix together the mince, the herbs, the beaten egg, the flour and the chilli flakes and onions in a bowl with a bit of salt and pepper.
3. Divide the mince evenly into about 6 portions and roll each portion into a ball in the palm of your hand – and then flatten and shape into 'burger size' to fit the buns.

These burgers are incredibly simple, way better than their supermarkets cousins and worth the extra effort. My son, Tom, makes brilliant burgers – and this is his recipe.

Satay sauce on page 220 and tomato ketchup are a must.

Serves 4-6

END

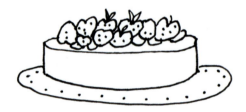

PUDDINGS AND DESSERTS

Apple Crumble

Baked Alaska

Baked Custard

Cheesecake

Chocolate Biscuit Cake

Chocolate Mousse

Fruit Strudel

Lemon Mousse

Speedy Lemon Flan

Summer Pudding

Raspberry Ice Cream

Raspberry Coulis

Warm Fruit Salad

White Chocolate and Raspberry Tart

APPLE CRUMBLE

Ingredients

5 large cooking apples
5 heaped tablespoons of flour
1 heaped tablespoon of porridge oats
3-4 heaped tablespoons of sugar (for the apples and the topping)
½ pack butter

Equipment

Hob
Oven: 190°C, 170°C fan and Gas Mark 5
Food processor or blender
Ovenproof dish or individual ramekins

■ Tips and Tricks

If there is topping left over – it freezes beautifully. I like plenty of topping so that it covers the fruit – and personally, I think a lot of recipes aren't generous enough.

This works just as well with any fruit – try apricots (tinned or fresh), plums, rhubarb or a handful of blackberries with the apples or a tablespoon of sultanas. Poach the fruit as above before adding the topping.

What to Do

1. Peel, core and slice the apples, and as you prepare each one, put them into a saucepan full of cold water to stop them going brown.
2. Drain off all but a mug full of water, add 1 or 2 tablespoons of sugar to taste and bring gently to simmering point and continue cooking for 2-3 minutes.
3. Take off the heat and keep the pan covered, so the apples continue to cook while you prepare the topping.
4. In a processor, combine the flour and the remaining sugar and butter until it resembles breadcrumbs. Add a bit more flour if it looks too 'sticky' and rub it in with your fingertips.
5. Fold in the porridge oats.
6. Put the apples in an ovenproof bowl, leave to cool for a while and then smooth the crumble mixture on top.
7. Put in the oven and bake for 30-35 minutes until bubbling and golden.

I think crumble looks great in individual ramekins and you can top each one with a dollop of vanilla ice cream, a spoonful of raspberry coulis (page 166) and some mint leaves.

Crumble is another one of the dishes that inspired me to dispense with the scales. My son, Tom, rang from abroad one night, asking for my crumble recipe. Rather than rifle through a cookery book – I made it up. This formula seemed to work for him and I hope it does for you too.

Serves 4-6

BAKED ALASKA

Ingredients

14 digestive biscuits
1/3 pack of butter – melted
1 large tub of vanilla ice cream – softened
4 egg whites
5 large tablespoons of caster sugar

Equipment

Oven: 220°C, 200°C fan, Gas Mark 7
Ovenproof flan dish – about 20 cm
Electric whisk

■ *Tips and Tricks*

If you want to prepare ahead, assemble the whole pudding, including the egg white topping and freeze it. Take it out of the freezer and leave it at room temperature for 10 minutes before putting it into the oven – and add an extra 2 or 3 minutes cooking time.

Don't be tempted to re-whisk the egg whites once they have taken shape – or they will separate.

What to Do

1. Crush the digestive biscuits in a blender, or put them into a clean cloth and bash with a rolling pin if you don't have a blender.
2. Melt the butter in a pan on a gentle heat and stir into the crushed biscuits.
3. Spread the biscuit mixture into the flan dish and flatten with your hands and allow to cool.
4. Put the softened ice cream into a mound on top of the biscuit base and return to the freezer while you prepare the meringue topping.
5. Whisk up the egg whites and sugar in a clean, dry pudding basin until it is forming soft peaks.
6. Take the ice cream out of the freezer and pile the meringue on top of the ice cream – making sure to seal it around the edges.
7. Bake for 5 minutes in the preheated, very hot oven until the meringue is just turning golden.

I prefer vanilla ice cream with this – but chocolate is equally delicious.

If you are in a 'chocolatey' sort of mood – substitute the plain digestive biscuits for chocolate digestive biscuits, the vanilla ice cream for chocolate ice cream, and you could even break up a few chocolate flakes onto the biscuit base underneath the ice cream.

Feel like going down the fruit route? *You can fold in a good few handfuls of raspberries into the ice cream – or scoop out the seeds from a couple of passion fruits.*

Serves 6

BAKED CUSTARD

Ingredients

Large carton of whipping cream (600 ml)
3 eggs
2 tablespoons of caster sugar
Few drops of vanilla essence

Equipment

Hob
Heatproof bowl
Electric whisk
Deep roasting tin
6 individual ramekin dishes
Oven: 180°C, 160°C fan, Gas Mark 3

■ Tips and Tricks

Simple, rich and creamy – this custard should be served at room temperature with stewed fruit – or best of all with Raspberry Coulis on page 166.

What to Do

1. Put the cream in a saucepan and bring it gently to simmering point – but don't boil it.
2. Whisk together the eggs and sugar in a bowl, pour the hot cream mixture on top, whisking continuously, and add the vanilla essence.
3. Pour into the individual ramekins.
4. Put the ramekin dishes in the deep roasting pan and fill with boiling water so that the water comes half way up the ramekin.
5. Bake for 20-25 minutes at 180°C, 160°C fan and Gas Mark 3, until the custard is still wobbly.

Serves 6

CHEESE CAKE

Ingredients

12/14 digestive biscuits
1/3 pack of butter
2 packs of soft cheese (about 400 g in all)
2 tablespoons of caster sugar
2 lemons (juice and zest)
4 tablespoons crème fraîche
1 egg
Mint for garnish – optional

Equipment

Loose-bottomed cake tin – about 23 cm
Oven: 180°C, 160°C fan, Gas Mark 4
Hob
Food processor

■ *Tips and Tricks*

It's best prepared in a blender but an electric mixer will do. Make sure the bowl is big enough, or you will end up redecorating the kitchen walls.

What to Do

1. Melt the butter in a pan.
2. Put the digestive biscuits in a processor and blend until crumbed and then mix into the melted butter.
3. Spread the biscuit mixture in the bottom of the tin and press down evenly with your hands.
4. Combine the soft cheese, caster sugar, juice of 2 lemons and zest of 1, crème fraîche and the egg in a processor and blend until smooth. Pour the cheese mixture onto the biscuit base.
5. Bake in the preheated oven for 30-35 minutes or until just setting. It should just 'wobble' slightly and it keeps cooking when it's out of the oven – so don't overdo it – or the surface will 'crack'.
6. Slide a knife around the edge of the tin and release the sides when it's cool.

This is a light cheesecake with a strong lemony flavour that offsets its richness. I love this with raspberry coulis on page 166.

If you have some fresh mint in stock – a tiny leaf on top makes it look even better.

Serves 6-8

END: PUDDINGS AND DESSERTS

CHOCOLATE BISCUIT CAKE

Ingredients

Half a pack of butter (approx. 125 g)
1 bar of milk chocolate (approx. 150 g)
1 bar of plain chocolate (approx. 150 g)
Medium pack of digestive biscuits (about 20)

Equipment

Hob
Loose-bottomed round cake tin (approx. 18 cm)
Heatproof basin

■ Tips and Tricks

If you don't have digestive biscuits – rich tea will do.
Lots of recipes list panforte as an addition. Personally, I don't like the combination of fruit and chocolate and much prefer digestive biscuits or rich tea.

What to Do

1 Put the butter and chocolate in a heatproof bowl over a pan of simmering water, and stir continuously until combined – this will take at least 5 minutes.
2 Crumble up the digestive biscuits into little pieces with your fingers or chop with a knife.
3 Add them to the chocolate mixture and stir in, until the biscuits are coated with the chocolate.
4 Pile the mixture into the cake tin and smooth down with your fingers to make an even surface and refrigerate for at least 2 hours.

Cut it into slices and all it needs is a dollop of vanilla ice cream. You can make this the day before – and it freezes beautifully too.

Serves 8-10

CHOCOLATE MOUSSE

Ingredients

    4 large whole eggs
    3 whites of eggs
    3 heaped tablespoons of caster sugar
    400g dark or milk chocolate or a mixture of the 2
    1 teaspoon of vanilla extract
    2 tablespoons of runny honey
    2 teaspoons of ground cinnamon
    Icing sugar to dust
    3 large tablespoons of double cream

Equipment

    4 heatproof bowls
    Electric whisk
    Large saucepan
    Hob
    4 wine glasses or small water glasses

Tips and Tricks

If you don't like the rich, less sugary taste of dark chocolate – use milk chocolate instead – or a combination of the 2, for a softer taste and paler colour.

It makes a mess with lots of bowls – but once you've cleared up and it's in the fridge – you can forget about it until you serve it. It will happily stay overnight in the fridge.

What to Do

1. Whisk the cream in a medium bowl until it forms soft peaks and set aside.
2. Put the whole eggs, the honey and 2 tablespoons of sugar (reserving 1 tablespoon) into another heatproof bowl.
3. Put the bowl over a large saucepan of simmering water and whisk continuously over gentle heat for about 10 minutes until it is thick and fluffy and set aside.
4. Wash and dry the whisk.
5. In another bowl, melt the chocolate and vanilla extract in the same pan of simmering water and when it is completely dissolved, with no lumps of chocolate, fold it into the egg mixture.
6. Meanwhile, whisk the egg whites in another clean, dry bowl, adding the remaining tablespoon of caster sugar, and beat until they form shiny, soft peaks.
7. Combine the whipped cream with the chocolate, the egg and honey mixture and then gently fold in the egg whites with a metal spoon. Give it a very quick whizz with the electric whisk to make sure the cream, egg whites and chocolate is combined.
8. Pour into the individual glasses and refrigerate for at least 2 hours before serving.
9. Sprinkle sieved icing sugar and cinnamon on top just before serving.

This is rich – so tiny portions are best.

Serves 4

FRUIT STRUDEL

Ingredients

1 pack of ready-made puff pastry
Handful of flour
1 pack of white marzipan – about 300 ml
Large pat of butter – melted
1 pack of frozen fruit – mixed berries or raspberries (defrosted)
1 large serving spoon of flaked almonds
1 dessertspoon of soft brown sugar

Equipment

Oven: 200°C, 180°C fan, Gas Mark 6
Large flat baking tray
Greaseproof paper
Baking beans

▌ Tips and Tricks

This might look a bit complicated; measuring the greaseproof paper and pastry. But there's no need to get out a set square and compass – just remember in descending order of size: baking tray, greaseproof paper, pastry and marzipan.

What to Do

1. Lightly poach the defrosted fruit, with a dessertspoon of sugar if you think it needs it, for 3-4 minutes until it is just bubbling – and set aside.
2. Cut a piece of greaseproof paper at least 40 cm long, sprinkle with flour.
3. Put the puff pastry on top, roll out with a rolling pin and then trim to roughly 30 cm x 15 cm rectangle.
4. Lift the pastry on the greaseproof paper and put it on a large baking tray, cover with another layer of greaseproof paper and top with the baking beans.
5. Put the baking tray into the preheated oven at 200°C, 180°C fan and Gas Mark 6.
6. Cook for about 12 minutes on the paper.
7. Remove from the oven and turn the temperature down to 170°C, 150°C fan and Gas Mark 3.
8. Lift off the top layer of greaseproof paper and baking beans (which will be very hot!).
9. Roll out the marzipan to a rectangle, half the width of the puff pastry and with a border on both ends of roughly 5cms and centre it on top of the puff pastry base.
10. Put the stewed fruit in the centre of the marzipan strip and roll up into a Swiss roll shape lengthways and tuck in the end edges and the central seam to seal the strudel.
11. Brush the strudel with the melted butter and then sprinkle the brown sugar on top.
12. Put the strudel in the oven and bake for 40 minutes.
13. Cover loosely with foil half way through if it looks as if it's getting too brown.

This can be made several hours ahead, or even the day before – and then stuck in the oven to heat through for 10 or 15 minutes just before serving.

Sprinkle with the almond flakes just before serving.

Serves 6

LEMON MOUSSE

Ingredients

3 large lemons
2 level teaspoons of gelatine
4 large eggs – separated
3 heaped tablespoons of caster sugar
Small carton of double cream (about 2/3 tablespoons)

Equipment

Hob
Electric whisk
4 individual ramekins or glasses
3 pudding basins

■ Tips and Tricks

Like the chocolate mousse on page 154, this is rich and you only need a small portion. I serve this in small straight sided glasses and garnish with curls of lemon peel, which you can do with a potato peeler.

What to Do

1. Finely grate one of the lemons and squeeze all 3.
2. Put the gelatine in a saucepan and sprinkle with 2 tablespoons of water, and heat very gently for a few minutes until the granules have dissolved and the liquid is clear.
3. Put the egg yolks in a bowl with the caster sugar and whisk for 2 or 3 minutes and then add the lemon juice, zest and the dissolved gelatine.
4. Stand the lemon mixture in a pan of iced water and whisk gently until it begins to thicken. Don't lose heart – this can take about 10 minutes.
5. Take it out of the water when it has thickened slightly and set aside.
6. In another bowl, whip the cream until it is just holding its shape and set aside.
7. Whisk the egg whites in another clean, dry bowl until they form peaks and then fold them into the lemon mixture until the egg whites are combined.
8. Give it a very quick whizz with the whisk to ensure all the ingredients are combined – but just for a second or 2, as you don't want to knock the air out of it.
9. Pour into the glasses and refrigerate for at least 3 hours or preferably overnight.

Despite the cream and sugar in this recipe, the lemon is beautifully 'tangy' and light.

I love this with raspberry coulis on page 166.

Serves 4

SPEEDY LEMON FLAN

Ingredients

10 ginger nut biscuits
⅓ pack of unsalted butter
4 lemons juiced – and zest of 1 lemon
Can of condensed milk (about 400 g)
3 tablespoons of double cream

Equipment

Hob
Electric whisk
Blender
Pudding basin
Flan dish (about 20 cm)

Tips and Tricks

Serve this on its own or with fresh fruit, raspberry coulis and a sprig of mint to jazz it up

What to Do

1. Melt the butter in a saucepan and set aside.
2. Crush the ginger biscuits in the blender.
3. Add the biscuits to the melted butter and combine.
4. Press the biscuit mixture into the bottom of the flan dish and squash down with your hands.
5. Set aside to cool.
6. Mix together the condensed milk, the lemon juice and zest and the cream with the electric whisk and whizz up until the mixture has thickened and pour on top of the biscuit base.
7. Chill for at least 2 or 3 hours and decorate with lemon zest just before serving.

Serves 4-6

END: PUDDINGS AND DESSERTS

SUMMER PUDDING

Ingredients

2 packs of frozen summer fruits – defrosted
2 Madeira cakes (ready-made)
1-2 tablespoons of caster sugar
Splash of brandy or cassis
Few sprigs of mint

Equipment

6 individual ramekins
Hob
Cling film

▮ Tips and Tricks

One Madeira cake is not quite enough to line the ramekins and 2 is too many – but eat what's left over with a cup of tea. I much prefer Madeira cake to white bread with this recipe.

The taste of British summer (hmmm)... this is easier than it looks, and a sprig of mint and a dollop of ice cream take it onto another level.

If you don't have ramekins – use a pudding basin instead.

What to Do

1. Line individual ramekins with cling film which helps when you come to tip the pudding out.
2. Cut the Madeira cake into thin slices and line the base and sides of the ramekins.
3. Defrost the fruit and poach gently with the sugar and liqueur, simmering for 2-3 minutes until the fruit is soft. Drain and reserve the cooking liquid.
4. Pour a little of the reserved liquid into the base of the ramekins so the cake soaks up the juices.
5. Fill the ramekins with the fruit and fold the cling film over the top to seal them and then refrigerate for at least 2 or 3 hours.
6. When you serve, tip each one onto a small plate and pour a little of the reserved cooking juice on top and decorate with a few leaves of mint.

I found this recipe quite hard to write so in a nutshell, line the ramekins with cling film and Madeira cake, poach the fruit, reserve the liquid, fill the ramekins with the fruit and fold over the cling film before refrigerating.

Crème fraîche or vanilla ice cream is all this needs.

Serves 6

RASPBERRY ICE CREAM

Ingredients

    2 packs of frozen raspberries – defrosted
    Juice of half an orange
    Medium pot of double cream – 10 tablespoons or 280 ml
    8 heaped tablespoons of icing sugar – sifted

Equipment

    Hob
    Freezer
    Pudding basin
    Plastic container for freezer
    Electric whisk

■ Tips and Tricks

I have never bothered getting an ice cream maker as I think they clutter up the kitchen cupboards – and this works just as well by stirring 3 or 4 times every 20 minutes – but of course, you can't go out and leave it until it's finished.

What to Do

1. Put the defrosted raspberries in a pan with the orange juice and cook for about 5 minutes.
2. Take them off the heat and pour off excess liquid.
3. Put the raspberries in a sieve, place on top of a pudding basin or bowl and press through with a wooden spoon to extract the purée.
4. Throw out the seeds left in the sieve.
5. Whip the cream until it is just holding its shape.
6. Sieve the icing sugar, and combine with the purée and the whipped cream.
7. Whisk until the mixture is combined.
8. Pour into a plastic container and put into the freezer.
9. After every 20 minutes, take the container out of the freezer and fork through, scraping the edges to the centre.
10. Repeat 2 or 3 more times to prevent crystals forming which will make the ice cream crunchy – not creamy.
11. When it is completely frozen, seal with a lid or cling film.
12. Take it out of the freezer 10 minutes before serving to soften slightly.

Serve with vanilla ice cream as a contrast of colours and flavours or fresh red fruits and – a few mint leaves. If you really want to go overboard on raspberry flavour – top with a spoonful of coulis on page 166.

Serves 8

RASPBERRY COULIS

Ingredients

1 pack of frozen raspberries or mixed fruit
Heaped tablespoon of icing sugar
Splash of port or brandy

Equipment

Hob
Sieve

■ Tips and Tricks

This adds an extra something to ice cream, natural yoghurt or baked custard (page 148) – and it's incredibly easy. I love the combination of raspberries with lemon puddings too – like the speedy lemon flan on page 160.

What to Do

1 Put the raspberries in a pan, pour over a tiny splash of brandy or port and set aside to defrost.
2 Bring gently to the boil and continue cooking until the fruit is pulpy for about 2/3 minutes, drain the raspberries and reserve the juice.
3 Put the raspberries in a sieve and squash them through with a wooden spoon over a pudding basin or dish to extract the purée.
4 Add the icing sugar to the purée and blend with a hand whisk to get rid of the lumps. If you want it slightly runnier, add a little of the reserved raspberry juice.

Serves 6-8

WARM FRUIT SALAD

Ingredients

A combination of any of these fruits – enough to fill a medium pudding basin

Strawberries

Nectarines

Peaches

Blackberries

Blackcurrants

Cherries – de-stoned

Syrup

1 tablespoon of caster sugar

5 tablespoons of red wine

2 tablespoons port

1 tablespoon of balsamic vinegar
1 orange (juiced)
Sprigs of mint for serving

Equipment

Heatproof serving bowl
Saucepan
Hob

Tips and Tricks

It's hard to be too prescriptive about the amount of fruit – but roughly go for a couple of large tablespoons for each person.

What to Do

1. Wash and prepare a selection of the above fruits – and put them into a heatproof serving bowl.
2. Mix together the caster sugar, red wine, port, balsamic vinegar and orange juice and heat until the sugar melts and then set aside – which can be done well in advance.
3. Just before serving, reheat the syrup almost to boiling point and then pour it over the fruit.

Soft summer fruits are so delicious with a winey syrup – and the balsamic vinegar may sound strange, but it gives the sauce real depth.

Serve this with natural yoghurt or ice cream.

Serves 6

WHITE CHOCOLATE AND RASPBERRY TART

Ingredients

1 pack ready-made sweet pastry – or ready-made sweet flan base
1 small tub mascarpone cheese (125 g)
Medium bar of white chocolate (about 200 g)
Large carton of double cream (400 g)
Fresh raspberries – about 400 g
1 tablespoon icing sugar – sifted

Equipment

Oven: 180°C, 160°C fan, Gas Mark 4
Baking beans
Electric whisk
20 cm loose-bottomed flan tin
Greaseproof paper
Heatproof bowl

■ *Tips and Tricks*

If you're short of time, buy a ready-made sweet flan base from a deli or supermarket which saves fiddling around with baking beans – and skip forward to preparing the filling.

What to Do

1. Roll out the pastry and line a 20 cm loose-bottomed flan tin.
2. Cover with greaseproof paper and baking beans, and bake in a preheated over 180°C, 160°C fan, Gas Mark 4 for 12-15 minutes.
3. Remove the paper and baking beans and bake for a further 5-10 minutes until the pastry is golden brown and 'crispy' and set aside to cool.
4. Put the mascarpone and white chocolate in a heatproof bowl over a pan of simmering water, and stir until the chocolate has melted.
5. Remove from the heat and leave to cool.
6. Whip the cream and fold the chocolate mixture into the cream, give it a quick whisk with the electric whisk and spoon into the pastry case. Push half of the raspberries into the chocolate, reserving the other half for decoration and refrigerate.
7. Just before serving, put the remaining raspberries on top and sieve the icing sugar on top.

I'm not normally a fan of fruit and chocolate together (particularly dark chocolate and orange) – but white chocolate and raspberries are the one exception. This is incredibly rich – nice for a treat – and it looks wonderful. Don't be stingy with the raspberries as they help to counteract the chocolaty base.

Serve 6-8

IN-BETWEEN

SALADS AND VEG

Bacon and Tomato Salad

Coleslaw

Honey and Lemon Couscous

Leek Gratin

Lots of Beans Salad

Mushy Peas

Potato and Celeriac Mash

Pumpkin with Lime and Yoghurt

Red Cabbage

Roasted Med Veg

Roasted Tomato and Mozzarella Salad

Rosemary and Garlic Roast Potatoes

Sesame Seed Salad

Spinach and Pesto Pasta

Tarragon Carrots

Tasty Rice

Tomato and Onion Relish

BACON AND TOMATO SALAD

Ingredients

6 eggs
12 rashers streaky bacon
12 cherry tomatoes
1 large handful of French beans
1 tablespoon of olive oil
1 dessertspoon of balsamic vinegar
1 teaspoon of grainy mustard
1 packet of washed, herby salad

Equipment

Hob
Frying pan

■ *Tips and Tricks*

Breakfast all day! Mop up the juices with hot, crusty bread.

What to Do

1. Hard boil the eggs for about 10 minutes and then plunge them into cold water for a few minutes.
2. Crack the shell – and run the eggs under the cold tap which makes them easier to peel.
3. Cook the French beans in boiling water for 2 minutes maximum or less if, like me, you like veg crispy not pappy.
4. Fry the bacon in a frying pan for about 3-4 minutes each side until crispy, and reserve the oil.
5. Chop the bacon into pieces and set aside.
6. Cut the tomatoes in half and add to the frying pan with the remains of the bacon fat and cook for a couple of minutes on both sides.
7. Whisk together the oil, vinegar, mustard and seasoning in a large salad bowl and add the salad, bacon and tomatoes, toss through the dressing and then top with the hard-boiled eggs, quartered.

Serves 4

COLESLAW

Ingredients

1 small crispy green cabbage – sliced
2-3 medium carrots – grated
2 tablespoons of sultanas
1 tablespoon of mayonnaise
2 tablespoons of natural yoghurt
1 lemon – juice and zest
Small bunch of parsley – chopped

Equipment

Food processor – for slicing

Tips and Tricks

Homemade coleslaw is as different as chalk and cheese to the flabby version that you can get in pubs that has come out of a tin. This is great with cold ham and peps up leftovers.

What to Do

1. Slice the green cabbage, if possible in a food processor.
2. Top, tail and peel the carrots and grate them.
3. Mix together the mayonnaise and yoghurt and add a squeeze of lemon juice and the zest.
4. Put the cabbage and carrots in a large bowl.
5. Stir in the sultanas, the mayonnaise and the yoghurt.
6. Have a taste and add a bit more mayo if you think it needs it.
7. Sprinkle with the chopped parsley.

Serves 6

HONEY AND LEMON COUSCOUS

Ingredients

2 mugs of couscous
Vegetable stock or boiling water (approx. 3 mugs)
½ cucumber – peeled and chopped
4 tomatoes – chopped
Large handful of mint
Large handful of coriander
1 tablespoon of runny honey
1 or 2 lemons – juiced

Equipment

Hob

Tips and Tricks

If you're fed up with pasta and rice – this is a little more work to prepare – but worth the effort. Worried about how much couscous to use – check the packet.

What to Do

1. Put the couscous into a heatproof basin and cover with boiling water or stock if you prefer.
2. 'Fluff up' with a fork after a few minutes.
3. Peel and chop the cucumber and squeeze off the excess liquid.
4. Chop the tomatoes and drain off the excess liquid to prevent the couscous becoming soggy.
5. Add the chopped mint, coriander, runny honey, tomatoes and cucumber to the couscous, together with a squeeze of lemon. Don't overdo the lemon juice or it will dominate rather than enhance the flavour.

Serves 6

LEEK GRATIN

Ingredients

6 medium leeks – cleaned and roughly chopped
2 medium carrots – grated
1 small glass of white wine
2 mugs of milk
1 tablespoon of chopped thyme
2 tablespoons of olive oil
¼ pack of butter
1 tablespoon of flour
3 tablespoons of grated Parmesan
4 heaped tablespoons of breadcrumbs

Equipment

Oven: 180°C, 160°C fan, Gas Mark 4
Hob
Wok or frying pan
Oven-proof dish

■ Tips and Tricks

The nicest breadcrumbs are the ones you make yourself. If you have a blender, just put in about 10 slices of white bread and whizz them up until they are coarse – don't make them too fine. What's left over freezes beautifully for the next time.

This dish can be made the day before – and just reheated for about 15/20 minutes until it's hot through.

What to Do

1. Trim, wash and roughly chop the leeks into bite-size pieces and grate the carrots.
2. Add the olive oil to the wok or frying pan and when just sizzling, add the leeks and carrots and sauté gently for about 10 minutes – stirring continuously to prevent scorching and sticking.
3. Add a small cube of butter from the pack (reserving the remainder for the sauce) and the glass of wine.
4. Continue cooking for another 5 minutes or so, until the liquid has just evaporated and transfer the mixture to an ovenproof dish.
5. Put the remaining butter in a pan and melt it gently.
6. Remove the pan from the heat and stir in the flour and when it's combined, add the milk.
7. Return the pan to the heat and continue stirring until the sauce begins to thicken.
8. Add half of the grated Parmesan, and continue cooking for another minute until it is bubbling gently.
9. Pour the sauce over the leeks.
10. Combine the remaining Parmesan with the breadcrumbs and sprinkle on top of the leeks.
11. Bake for about 30 minutes in the oven until the top is golden and the sauce is bubbling.

Team this with roast chicken, beef or lamb or just on its own as a light meal.

Serves 6

LOTS OF BEANS SALAD

Ingredients

2 tins of lentils
2 tins of kidney beans
1 can of sweet corn
1 can of cannellini beans
Large handful of dried apricots – chopped
Bunch of spring onions – chopped
Bunch of coriander – chopped
2 courgettes – finely chopped
1 tablespoon of olive oil

For the Dressing

1 tablespoon of balsamic vinegar
2 tablespoons of olive oil
2 cloves of garlic

Equipment

Hob
Can opener

Tips and Tricks

Don't dress the salad until an hour before serving – or it will go soggy.

What to Do

1. Drain and rinse the tins of beans and corn, and pile them all into a large salad bowl.
2. Heat 1 tablespoon of the oil in a frying pan, and add the spring onions and courgettes and fry until just softened for about 5 minutes and combine with the beans.
3. Add the chopped coriander and apricots to the beans and vegetables.
4. Mix the dressing ingredients: the remaining olive oil (2 tablespoons), balsamic vinegar and garlic in a screw topped jar and shake well to combine and toss into the beans and vegetables.

Got a tin opener? Then you're on course for a delicious salad as a main course or a side dish. You can ring the changes with any canned beans in the cupboard.

Serves 6-8

MUSHY PEAS

Ingredients

1 medium pack of frozen peas (about 400 g)
Large bunch of spring onions
1 dessertspoon of olive oil
Generous scoop of butter
2 or 3 tablespoons of water
1 tablespoon of single cream
½ teaspoon of sugar
Salt and pepper

Equipment

Blender
Hob

■ Tips and Tricks

If you are cooking this ahead and then reheating, make sure you cover it with cling film and refrigerate. Remove the cling film and heat gently just before serving.

What to Do

1. Heat a pan gently with the oil and butter and add the washed and chopped spring onions and cook for 5 minutes until soft.
2. Add the frozen peas, water and sugar and bring to simmering point, and continue cooking for another 4/5 minutes.
3. Add the cream and put the mixture into a food processor and whiz until it's still coarse but not completely puréed.
4. Have a taste – and add a bit of salt and pepper if it needs a boost.
5. Serve immediately, or allow to cool. Reheat gently when required.

This is so easy and goes with everything from a Sunday roast to boeuf bourguignon.

Serves 4-6

POTATO AND CELERIAC MASH

Ingredients

6 medium potatoes – peeled and chopped
½ medium celeriac – peeled and chopped
2 tablespoons of single cream
2 teaspoons of grainy mustard
Generous scoop of butter

Equipment

Hob
Ovenproof dish
Oven: 200°C, 180°C fan, Gas Mark 5

Tips and Tricks

This is even better made the day before. Cover it with foil, cool and refrigerate. To reheat, put the covered dish into the preheated medium oven for 20 minutes, remove the foil and heat up for another 10 minutes so it is slightly crispy on top. Peel the celeriac like a spud and cut into pieces. Put in less celeriac if you don't want it overpowering the potato.

What to Do

1. Cook the potatoes and celeriac until tender for about 15 minutes.
2. Drain and mash with the butter, cream and mustard and a bit of salt and pepper if it needs it.
3. Put in an ovenproof dish, cover with foil and heat in the oven for 20 minutes.
4. Check the dish is hot through, remove the foil and cook for a further 10 minutes for a crispy crust.

Simply peel the celeriac like a spud – cutting it into quarters makes it easier – put in less if you don't want it dominating the potato.

Serves 4-6

IN-BETWEEN: SALADS AND VEG

PUMPKIN WITH LIME AND YOGHURT

Ingredients

1 small pumpkin
3-4 tablespoons of olive oil
Small pot of natural yoghurt
Juice and zest of 1 lime
Handful of parsley – chopped

Equipment

Roasting tin
Oven: 200°C, 180°C fan, Gas Mark 5

■ Tips and Tricks

No pumpkin – then use butternut squash or sweet potatoes.

Roasting the pumpkin brings out the sweetness of the veg and the lime and yoghurt mixture is a good contrast to the sweetness. This is delicious and perfect with something simple like roast chicken, beef or salmon.

Don't prepare this more than an hour before you serve it – or the yoghurt goes a bit dry.

What to Do

1. Leave the skin on the pumpkin, cut into quarters, scoop out the seeds and cut into 'bite-size' chunks.
2. Put into the preheated oven on a roasting tray, drizzle a generous glug (about 3-4 tablespoons) of olive oil and salt and pepper and roast for about 30 to 40 minutes until just turning golden.
3. Put in a serving dish and allow to cool slightly.
4. Combine the yoghurt and lime juice, and pour in blobs over the pumpkin and leave at room temperature for the flavours to be absorbed.
5. Sprinkle with the chopped parsley just before serving.

Serves 4-6

RED CABBAGE

Ingredients

2 tablespoons of olive oil
Generous scoop of butter
1 medium red cabbage – shredded
2 large onions – peeled and chopped
1-2 tablespoons of soft brown sugar (according to taste)
2 medium cooking apples – peeled, cored and sliced
1-2 tablespoons of red wine vinegar
1 lemon – squeezed

Equipment

Large saucepan
Hob
Food processor or grater

Tips and Tricks

You can make this ahead – refrigerate and reheat just before serving. And it actually improves with a bit of maturity.

What to Do

1. Heat the oil and butter in a pan and fry the onions for about 5 minutes before adding the remaining ingredients: the cabbage, sugar, vinegar, apples and a squeeze of lemon.
2. Cover with a lid and simmer very gently on the hob for about half an hour – if you like it with a bit of bite – or another half an hour if you like it slightly softer. But keep checking it, so it doesn't dry out.
3. During the cooking, taste and add a bit more salt, sugar and vinegar if you think it needs it.

This is traditionally a Christmas dish – but it goes wonderfully with chicken or ham all year round.

Serves 6-8

ROASTED MED VEG

Ingredients

4 courgettes
1 aubergine
3 onions
2 red/yellow peppers
1 or 2 fennel bulbs – optional
2 tablespoons of olive oil

Equipment

Roasting tin
Oven: 200°C, 180°C fan, Gas Mark 6

■ *Tips and Tricks*

If your fridge yields fewer courgettes, more peppers or a stray sweet potato – go for it. Don't overcrowd the roasting tin or the veg will steam, not roast.

What to Do

1. Slice the aubergine and sprinkle with salt on both sides to make it 'sweat' for about 10 minutes each side. Dab with kitchen roll which takes out any bitterness.
2. Top and tail the courgettes, onions and peppers and slice them roughly.
3. If you're using fennel, cut off the base and divide them into quarters, vertically.
4. Put a roasting tin in a preheated oven and add an extra splash of oil to the tin. When it's hot, add the veg and sprinkle sparingly with salt and pepper.
5. Roast in the oven for 50 minutes or until they are just beginning to tinge.

I have great memories of eating Roasted Med Veg when my family lived in Greece. The veg were all different shapes and sizes but tasted wonderful and a million times better than the 'perfect' specimens that grace the supermarket shelves.

Serves 4-6

ROASTED TOMATO AND MOZZARELLA SALAD

Ingredients

1 tablespoon of olive oil
1 lemon – zest and juice
4 ripe beef tomatoes or 8 medium tomatoes
Basil leaves
2 medium balls of mozzarella
Tin anchovies – optional

For the Dressing

2 tablespoons of olive oil
1 tablespoon of balsamic vinegar
1 clove of garlic

Equipment

Medium Grill

Tips and Tricks

The dullest tomatoes come to life when they're roasted – and this is great either as a starter or a light lunch.

What to Do

1. Preheat grill and line the grill pan with foil.
2. Cut the tomatoes in half and brush both sides with olive oil, the zest of lemon and a good grind of salt and pepper. Grill for 4 or 5 minutes on both sides until they are just beginning to soften.
3. Remove from the grill and put a slice of mozzarella on the tomatoes and return to the grill for about 3 minutes or until the cheese is just beginning to bubble.
4. Shake ingredients for the dressing in a screw-topped jar and season.
5. Put the tomatoes and mozzarella slices on individual side plates and top with the anchovies (if you're using them).
6. Drizzle over the dressing and scatter the torn up basil leaves on top.

Serves 4 as a main or 8 as a starter

ROSEMARY AND GARLIC ROASTED POTATOES

Ingredients

8-10 medium potatoes – washed and quartered
8-10 baby onions – peeled
2 cloves garlic – crushed
3-4 sprigs rosemary
2 tablespoons oil
½ teaspoon salt

Equipment

Roasting pan
Oven: 200°C, 180°C fan, Gas Mark 6

Tips and Tricks

These potatoes are great with roasts or any barbequed meat. They're easy to prepare – and just need a quick flip over half way through cooking so they don't stick irrevocably to the pan.

What to Do

1. Don't waste time peeling the potatoes – they're better cooked in their skins – just wash them and cut into halves or quarters.
2. Mix together the olive oil, crushed garlic and salt in a bowl and coat the potatoes and onions with the oil.
3. Heat the oven and put another glug of olive oil in the roasting pan. When it's sizzling, add the coated potatoes and throw in the rosemary (keep 1 sprig for garnish) – stripping the leaves off the sprigs and roast for about an hour, until golden brown.

Serves 4

SESAME SEED SALAD

Ingredients

½ cucumber
1 red pepper
1 yellow pepper
6 spring onions – chopped roughly
12 cherry tomatoes – halved
1 lime – zest and juice
2 teaspoons of runny honey
1 tablespoon of grainy mustard
Handful of chopped mint
1 dessertspoon of sesame seeds

■ Tips and Tricks

This is a fantastic, fresh-tasting salad that goes particularly well with the Chilli Salmon Fishcakes on page 64 and the dressing is oil free.

What to Do

1 Cut the cucumber into roughly 20 cm slices and then cut them lengthways into fairly fine strips.
2 Deseed the peppers and cut them into thin slices, combine them with the cucumber, chopped spring onions and the halved cherry tomatoes and put them in a salad bowl.
3 Mix together the lime juice and zest with the honey and grainy mustard and pour it over the salad.
4 Sprinkle with the sesame seeds and the chopped mint.

Serves 4

TARRAGON CARROTS

Ingredients

10 large carrots – peeled and sliced
Large scoop of butter
½ teaspoon of caster sugar
1 lemon – zest and juice
1 tablespoon of chopped tarragon
Splash of single cream

Equipment

Hob

■ Tips and Tricks

This dish is perfect with a roast – but it's just a bit more complicated on timing – the carrots don't take kindly to being kept waiting. To ring the changes, swap the lemon for a squeeze of half an orange and a bit of zest.

What to Do

1 Boil the carrots for 5 minutes or a bit longer if you don't like them 'al dente', drain them and keep warm.
2 Melt the butter in a pan, add the carrots, caster sugar, lemon zest, lemon juice and the splash of cream.
3 Stir in the chopped tarragon just before serving.

I love the combination of tarragon, cream and a squeeze of lemon with the carrots. This perks up even the dullest carrots, but of course, with organic carrots – it's the best.

Serves 4-6

TASTY RICE

Ingredients

1 mug of rice
2 tablespoons of olive oil
2 large onions – chopped
3-4 rashers of bacon – chopped
1-2 mugs of frozen peas
2 mugs of vegetable stock
1 tablespoon of soy sauce

Equipment

Hob
Frying Pan
Saucepan

■ *Tips and Tricks*

This is great for pepping up something as simple as grilled sausages or roast chicken and it's a bit more interesting than plain rice.

What to Do

1. Peel and chop the onions.
2. Cook the rice for half the time recommended on the packet and drain it before it is completely cooked.
3. Heat the oil in the frying pan, and when it's hot, add the onions and the bacon and fry for about 5 minutes, until they are beginning to soften and turn slightly golden.
4. Put the half-cooked rice into the frying pan with the onions and bacon, add the stock and soy sauce and continue cooking for another 5 or 10 minutes, until the rice is beginning to absorb the stock.
5. Add the peas, from frozen, to the rice mixture and continue cooking for another 5 minutes, or until all the stock is absorbed and the peas are hot through.
6. Add another splash of soy if it needs more flavour and a bit more stock.

My children called this 'Tasty Rice' when they were little – and all 3 of them loved it (and still do).

Serves 4

SAUCES

Apple and Mustard Sauce

Béarnaise Sauce with Tarragon

Cheese Sauce

Exceedingly Easy Parsley Sauce

Guacamole

Hollandaise Sauce

Liz's Mango Salsa

Mushroom Sauce

Onion Gravy

Port and Cranberry Sauce

Red Onion and Tomato Relish

Red Pepper Sauce

Satay Sauce

Tartar Sauce

Tomato Sauce

Tzatziki

APPLE AND MUSTARD SAUCE

Ingredients

4 large cooking apples
Zest and juice of ½ lemon
1 dessertspoon of caster sugar
1 teaspoon of grainy mustard

Equipment

Hob

■ Tips and Tricks

When you peel the apples, keep them completely covered in water to prevent them going brown – and drain off all but a few glasses of water when you start cooking them.

What to Do

1 Put the apples, juice of the lemon, the zest and sugar into the pan with a few glasses of water.
2 Bring to simmering point and continue cooking for about 5 minutes.
3 Take off the heat and leave it to stand with the lid on to finish cooking.
4 Drain the excess liquid if it looks too runny.
5 This is the perfect partner for pork or ham, or leave out the mustard, and serve it with ice cream or yoghurt.

Serves 6

BÉARNAISE SAUCE WITH TARRAGON

Ingredients

½ pack of unsalted butter
3 egg yolks
2 shallots – finely chopped
2/3 tablespoons of white wine vinegar
1 bunch of tarragon
Cube of ice – at the ready

Equipment

Hob
Electric whisk
Large saucepan
Heatproof pudding basin

■ Tips and Tricks

This sauce is a must with barbequed steaks or lamb chops. If it 'curdles' and looks like scrambled egg – just add a small cube of ice – which works wonders and has the miraculous effect of 'decurdling' it. Take the ice cube out when it's done its job, or the sauce goes too watery. I add another egg yolk if this happens and keep whisking until it's the right consistency

What to Do

1. Chop the shallots and put them in a pan with 2-3 tablespoons of white wine vinegar.
2. Bring the vinegar to simmering point and continue heating for 2 or 3 minutes, or until the liquid has reduced by half.
3. Drain the remaining liquid from the shallots and set aside.
4. Melt the butter and set aside.
5. Separate the white and yolks from the eggs and put the yolks into a heatproof pudding basin.
6. Boil the kettle.
7. Put the pudding basin with the yolks into a saucepan half filled with the boiling water.
8. Put it on a gentle heat and whisk continuously until the eggs are just beginning to thicken.
9. Pour in the melted butter, a drizzle at a time, until it's combined – at this point add a tiny bit of the vinegar at a time – tasting as you go. Don't overdo the vinegar or the sauce becomes too sharp.
10. Add the chopped tarragon just before serving.

This is another 'time-sensitive' recipe. If you are barbequing – you definitely need someone to keep their eye on the ball with the steaks while you concentrate on the Béarnaise – you can't do both!

Serves 4-6

CHEESE SAUCE

Ingredients

¼ pack of butter
2 dessertspoons of flour
2 mugs of milk (about 500 ml)
2-3 tablespoons of grated Cheddar cheese (or Parmesan)

Equipment

Hob
Saucepan

■ Tips and Tricks

This is so easy – but don't go into meltdown if it looks lumpy – just tip the sauce into a sieve and bash out the lumps with a wooden spoon.

What to Do

1. Melt the butter gently in a saucepan.
2. Take the pan off the heat and stir in the flour.
3. When it's combined, return to the heat and add the milk and the cheese, stirring continuously until it's combined.
4. Continue cooking slowly and stirring for another 5 minutes until the sauce has thickened and is just simmering. Add another splash of milk if it looks too thick.

When I'm making this sauce for lasagne – I normally double up the quantities.

Serves 4

EXCEEDINGLY EASY PARSLEY SAUCE

Ingredients

¼ pack of unsalted butter (about 50 g)
2 dessertspoons of flour
2 mugs of milk
Large bunch of parsley

Equipment

Blender
Hob

Tips and Tricks

This sauce is all the better for being made the day before which gives the parsley time to infuse into the milk. Just keep it in the fridge and heat it up gently before you need it.

What to Do

1. Put the butter, flour and milk in the blender and whizz it up for about 30 seconds.
2. Add the parsley and whizz for not more than 15 seconds – so the parsley is chopped not pulped.
3. Put the mixture on a gentle heat on the hob and bring to simmering point – by that time all the lumps will have disappeared.

Gammon isn't gammon without parsley sauce and broad beans.

Serves 4

GUACAMOLE

Ingredients

2 ripe avocados
3-4 spring onions
3 large tomatoes – skinned
2 limes – juiced
2 tablespoons of olive oil
2 tablespoons of chopped fresh coriander
1 green chilli – finely chopped and deseeded

Equipment

Heatproof pudding basin

■ Tips and Tricks

If you are not serving the guacamole immediately, cover and seal with cling film to prevent discolouring, and refrigerate.

This is a perfect partner to chilli con carne or just served with pita bread.

What to Do

1 Put the tomatoes in a heatproof pudding basin, pour over boiling water, prick the skins with a fork and leave for 1 minute.
2 Carefully take the tomatoes out of the hot water – the skins should come off easily with a knife.
3 Take the core out of the tomatoes and chop them roughly.
4 Squeeze out the excess liquid with your hands or put them in a sieve.
5 Cut the avocados in half, remove the stones, mash them up roughly and then add the chopped spring onions, olive oil, coriander, lime juice and chilli.

Serves 6

HOLLANDAISE SAUCE

Ingredients

3 egg yolks
White of 1 egg
⅓ pack of unsalted butter
2 lemons – squeezed

Equipment

Electric whisk
Hob
2 heatproof pudding basins

▌ Tips and Tricks

This is a lighter version of Béarnaise Sauce on page 204. While the 2 sauces are close cousins, I think this Hollandaise is perfect with English asparagus when it's in season or with Eggs Benedict for brunch, and the Béarnaise Sauce goes best with meat or chicken.

As with Béarnaise Sauce, keep an ice cube at the ready and drop it into the sauce if it begins to curdle.

What to Do

1. Separate the yolks and whites from the eggs – keeping 3 egg yolks and the white of 1 egg.
2. Put the butter in a pan and melt it slowly on the hob. Take care not to let it go brown – or it will taste bitter and discolour the sauce – and set aside.
3. Squeeze the lemons and whizz up the egg yolks with the electric whisk in a heatproof pudding basin over a saucepan of simmering water until it's just beginning to thicken.
4. Continue whisking and slowly pour in the melted butter, a little at a time until it is combined.
5. Take the basin off the heat.
6. Meanwhile, whisk the white of 1 of the eggs with a clean, dry whisk until it forms peaks.
7. Fold the egg white, a spoonful at a time into the warm egg yolk mixture and add a bit of salt and pepper if it needs it and a bit more lemon juice if you want the sauce a bit sharper. Give it a very quick whizz to combine the yolks and the white and serve immediately.

Serves 4-6

LIZ'S MANGO SALSA

Ingredients

2 large and very ripe mangoes
Bunch of coriander (chopped)
Bunch of spring onions (sliced)
1 dessertspoon of sweet chilli dipping sauce
1 lime – juice and zest

Tips and Tricks

This is so quick to throw together – and is particularly good with Harissa Lamb on page 106 and great with chicken or pork kebabs.

What to Do

1 Peel and slice the mangoes and put in a non-metallic bowl.
2 Add the chopped coriander, sliced spring onions, sweet chilli dipping sauce and the juice and zest of the lime.

I've named this Liz's Mango Salsa. My sister, Liz, loves it, but keeps asking for the recipe. She will have to buy my book next time she wants it!

Serves 6

MUSHROOM SAUCE

Ingredients

1 large onion – finely chopped
8 medium mushrooms – sliced
2 cloves of garlic – crushed
1 dessertspoon of flour
1 tablespoon of olive oil
Scoop of butter
1 glass of white wine
2 tablespoons of crème fraîche
½ veg stock cube – dissolved in ½ mug of water
Handful of fresh thyme or tarragon – chopped
Grated Parmesan

Equipment

Hob
Saucepan

Tips and Tricks

This sauce peps up any grilled meat or chicken – and it's great on top of pasta with some grated Parmesan.

What to Do

1. Heat the oil and butter in the pan and throw in the onions and cook gently for about 5 minutes until just beginning to soften.
2. Add the mushrooms and garlic and continue cooking for another few minutes, take the pan off the heat and stir in the flour.
3. Pour in the white wine, return to the hob, bring slowly to simmering point and carry on cooking until the sauce is beginning to thicken.
4. Dissolve the stock cube in boiling water and allow to cool for a few minutes before adding to the sauce.
5. Stir in the crème fraîche and herbs – and check the seasoning. Sprinkle with the grated Parmesan.

Serves 4

ONION GRAVY

Ingredients

2 medium onions – finely chopped
1 tablespoon of olive oil
1 teaspoon of runny honey
1 tablespoon of flour
1 tablespoon of balsamic vinegar
1 wineglass of red wine
1 stock cube – beef or vegetable
Small handful of herbs – thyme, rosemary or tarragon

Equipment

Hob
Saucepan

▍*Tips and Tricks*

This is onion gravy like Granny made it – and it's just great with sausages and mash.

What to Do

1. Heat the oil in the pan and when it's sizzling, add the chopped onion and cook for a good 5 minutes until it's beginning to soften.
2. Take off the heat and stir in the flour, balsamic vinegar, honey, crumbled stock cube, red wine and herbs.
3. Return it to the heat, bring gently to simmering point and then add a mug or water.
4. Keep stirring and then check it's the consistency you like. If it looks too thick – add a little more water.

Serves 4-6

PORT AND CRANBERRY SAUCE

Ingredients

3 tablespoons of cranberry jelly
1 tablespoon of port
1 teaspoon of Dijon mustard

Equipment

Hob

Tips and Tricks

If you don't have cranberry sauce – this works just as well with redcurrant jelly.

What to Do

1 Put the cranberry or redcurrant jelly, port and mustard in a pan and heat for 3-4 minutes until the jelly has dissolved.

Another facelift for roast chicken or lamb or cold ham – and it's so easy. You can also add some chopped fresh mint while you're heating it up.

TOMATO AND ONION RELISH

Ingredients

1 red onion, finely chopped
3 tomatoes, diced
1 tablespoon of mint, chopped
Juice of ½ a lime
Pinch of sugar

▌Tips and Tricks

This goes with any cold meat but, in particular, is a great accompaniment to the Lamb Korma on page 110.

What to Do

1 Mix all the ingredients together in a bowl and check for seasoning.

Serves 4-6

RED PEPPER SAUCE

Ingredients

2 onions – chopped
1 jar of red peppers – drained and roughly chopped
1 large mug of passata
1 dessertspoon of olive oil
1 tablespoon of sun-dried tomato paste
Splash of water
½ teaspoon of hot chilli pepper flakes (optional)

Equipment

Blender
Hob

Tips and Tricks

This perks up fish or meat – and is great on its own with pasta and some shaved Parmesan. Add hot chilli flakes if you want it punchier.

What to Do

1 Heat the olive oil in a pan, add the chopped onions and cook gently for 5 minutes.
2 Stir in the drained, chopped red peppers, sun-dried tomato paste and passata, a splash of water and the chilli flakes if you're using them.
3 Cook gently for 10 minutes and then put the mixture in a food processor and whiz until smooth.

Serves 4

SATAY SAUCE

Ingredients

3 heaped tablespoons of peanut butter
1 tablespoon of Thai red curry paste
½ can of coconut milk
6 tablespoons of hot water
Squeeze of lemon or lime juice

Equipment

Hob
Saucepan

■ Tips and Tricks

I prefer this with smooth peanut butter – but use crunchy if that's what you have in stock. It's delicious with any barbequed meats: chicken, steak, lamb or fish. Love it.

What to Do

1. Put the peanut butter in a saucepan and add 6 tablespoons of hot water and heat gently until the water has mixed with the peanut butter.
2. Add the Thai curry paste and coconut milk to the pan and bring just to simmering point until all the ingredients are combined.
3. Add a squeeze of lemon juice.
4. Serve at room temperature or slightly warmed.

This is ready in minutes and can be made the day before and heated up gently. The addition of hot water helps the sauce to combine.

Serves 4-6

TARTARE SAUCE

Ingredients

2 tablespoons of mayonnaise
1 dessertspoon capers – drained
8 baby gherkins
2-3 spring onions (chopped roughly)
Handful of parsley
1 tablespoon of olive oil
1 tablespoon of natural yoghurt
Squeeze of lemon juice

Equipment

Blender

Tips and Tricks

This classic mayonnaise-based sauce gives a hit that sharpens up grilled fish or fishcakes and is so much nicer than ready-made tartare sauce, and good quality mayonnaise does the job just fine. Cut down on the mayonnaise and increase the yoghurt if you like it less sharp.

What to Do

1. Put all the ingredients in a blender.
2. Whizz together but don't overdo it – the mixture should have a 'bite'.

Serves 4-6

TOMATO SAUCE

Ingredients

2 onions
1 clove of garlic, crushed
Splash of olive oil
5-6 fresh tomatoes (skinned and chopped)
1 tablespoon sun-dried tomato paste or tomato purée
1 cup of tomato passata
Pinch of sugar

Equipment

Hob
Heatproof pudding basin

Tips and Tricks

The goes-with-anything sauce – pile on top of pasta or serve it alongside chicken, fish or meat. Add a teaspoon of chilli flakes for heat or a tablespoon each of capers and pitted olives for a more Mediterranean flavour.

What to Do

1. Put the tomatoes in a heatproof dish and pour over boiling kettle water – pierce them with a knife and leave for a few minutes until the skin is just falling off.
2. Remove the tomatoes carefully from the basin and roughly chop them on a board – cutting out the core.
3. Heat the oil in a pan, add the peeled, chopped onions and fry gently for 3-4 minutes and then stir in the crushed garlic and chopped tomatoes.
4. Add the passata and sun-dried tomato paste, a pinch of sugar and simmer slowly for 10-15 minutes.

Serves 4-6

TZATZIKI

Ingredients

½ large tub of natural yoghurt
1-2 cloves of garlic
Large handful of mint (chopped)
¼ cucumber (chopped finely or grated)
½ lemon – squeezed
Salt and pepper

Equipment

Grater

■ *Tips and Tricks*

Leave out the garlic if you don't want to have 'garlic breath' the next day!

What to Do

1. Grate or finely chop the cucumber and squeeze out the excess liquid by hand.
2. Combine all the ingredients in a bowl and check for seasoning.
3. Refrigerate and garnish with a sprig of mint.

Way better than anything you'll find in the supermarket – this is brilliant with barbeques or any grilled meat or with toasted pita bread for dipping.